Förlag: BoD – Books on Demand, Stockholm, Sverige
Tryck: BoD – Books on Demand, Norderstedt,
Tyskland ISBN: 978-91-8027-854-6

"Know Your Self"

And Your Inter-Subjective Realities

Staffan Garpebring

Table of content

Preface

Writing this book gave me the opportunity to process the experiences I gained working in a host of different settings including schools, within child psychiatry, habilitation, mental care of teens and young adults and primary health care facilities.

Three overarching themes are interwoven in the book:

1. Understanding personal feelings and actions.
2. Reviewing the history of psychology and psychotherapy.
3. Presentation of the modus operandi I use as a psychologist.

The aim of the book is to integrate certain aspects of object relation therapy and gestalt therapy in a behavioral science context. In other words, to describe a dynamic, systematic inter-subjective theory.

I will not address personality disorders in depth. The book is about connecting with oneself and understanding personal feelings in order to ensure an authentic interaction with others. In this book, I want to look at two new concepts: FRAMES-analysis and FRAMES-dissonance.

The ability to relate to others is a challenge and can vary in difficulty depending on how smooth or rocky our relationships in early life were.

The psychosomatic FRAMES-model:

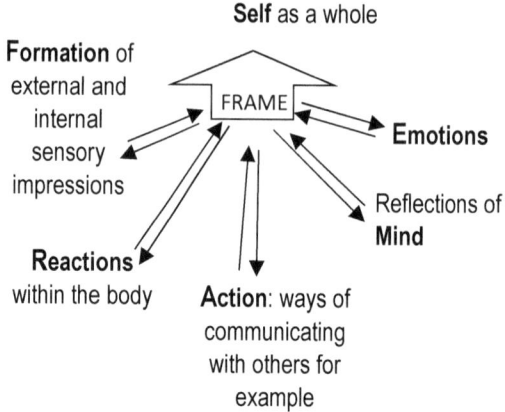

The concept of FRAMES, which I outline in this book is intended to describe the dynamic interaction between body and soul within the cultural setting.

If Freud were alive today, he would surely concur that the "super-ego" is the instantiation within us of a moral code that is developed through our experience of ourselves within our own social environment. The super-ego has evolved through the interaction between our genetic make-up and how we perceive and react to the experiences we have within the particular cultural environment in which we live.

I imagine that Freud and I would have been in agreement that the "id" incorporates what we understand to be the body.

Furthermore, I suspect that we would have agreed that the "ego" is formed, to greater or lesser extent, of conscious mental reflections upon that which we concentrate our attention (selectively targeted attention). Conversely, this process banishes thoughts that we don't focus on to the realms of the subconscious or may even render them totally unconscious.

After writing the original edition of this book with the Swedish title "Vetande om sig själv", I listened to Yuval Harari's *Homo Deus* (Swedish Audio Book).

Harari's reasoning in his book, gave me solace in my conviction that humans, throughout their history, have created different concepts about morality, divinity and immortality, in order to find meaning and purpose in life.

Fictional concepts, that have been established and won a universal and incontrovertible measure of value in contemporary life, such as the suggested morals of the gods or the importance assigned to money as the embodiment of material value even though they are only pieces of paper or the binary code of cyber currency, have a great impact on human interaction, and in society at large, but only as long as the individuals that make up society believe in these ideas.

When people collectively adopt a belief system, those beliefs become a part of their inter-subjective reality.

Accordingly, the subjective reality must then be squared off with the objective reality that people truly experience.

These realities interact in a mutual dynamic process whereby people's conceptual world must be brought to terms with their own perception of the extrinsic and intrinsic sensory impressions that they actually experience in everyday life.

Yuval Harari's and my own book theoretecize about the concepts of consciousness and soul.

Special thanks to Joe Sinnott whose co-operation in translating this text from Swedish to English, has allowed me to find the right words to illustrate the functioning of the psyche as a dynamic system, involving both intra and inter-individual dimensions.

Introduction

While I was studying to become a psychologist, I never once remember my tutors relating to the word "soul".

The soul is a central concept within theology and philosophy. Freud chose the Greek word psyche as a central tenet in his conception of a scientific doctrine about the soul and a constituent part of his framework for therapeutic discussion.

The concept of FRAMES, which I outline in this book is intended to describe the dynamic interaction between body, soul and culture.

Professor Yuval Harari's reasoning in his book gave me solace in my conviction that humans have created abstract concepts about divinity and morality in order to find meaning and purpose in life.

The cognitive advances made by homo sapiens during their evolution made it possible for them to come to agreement on and communicate ever more abstract concepts about earlier generations and divinities.

This provided an ideal environment for the proliferation of *inter-subjective* networks, i.e., means of socializing within particular cultural circumstances.

Towns and kingdoms, social classes, religious celebrations and ceremonies, sub-cultures and widespread cultural systems developed.

People could discuss, in subjectively recognizable and relatable terms, the abstract concepts of the morals and divine powers of the gods.

Trade and commerce necessitated the development of pictorial and written symbols capable of relating abstract thoughts in a manner that could be understood by all.

Fictitious concepts allowing us to assign value to implicitly worthless materials such as coins and notes or to the binary code of computers to represent value as digital currency, show us how contemporary man believes in and accepts as irrefutable, these inter-subjective realities in their dealings with each other.

Inter-subjective realities (sub-cultures and generally pervasive cultures) within the societal institutions, religion, politics, economy, social media and so on, influence people's inter-subjective interactions. They influence people's interactions irrespective of how aware, or not, these individuals are of those abstract beliefs that prevail in the culture to which they belong.

Inter-subjective realities (opinions and moral values), that are predominantly confirmed and consolidated in spoken language, choice of words, mimicry and tone of voice, have a great influence, not only on our inter-personal relationships but even on our constitutional make-up (intra-personally).

People's inter-subjective realities can present in a wide variety of individual forms.

Both Yuval Harari's book and this book, philosophize about the abstract concept of the soul from various vantage points.

As a psychologist, I have found it to be a considerable challenge to reconcile the difference between the introverted perspective of the soul prevalent within object relations theory and the more observational, extroverted perspective within psychotherapy.

The soul, the essence of being, is itself an abstraction of the wholeness of what we are as human-beings; our thoughts, feelings, actions and reactions in given circumstances. That wholeness includes both our own experience from within ourselves as well as the external perspective of others.

The body and soul are inseparable. They are mutually inter-dependent and experienced in unison.

The body including the brain is the concrete, basic requirement for the soul to exist in our earthly lives.

In this book, my ambition has been to problematize the fact that the soul, in many contexts, ever since René Descartes time, has been seen as a separate entity from the body and that it goes on after our corporal demise.

The body´s importance for the soul and our well-being is, alas, something that we are, more or less, oblivious to.

Similarly, we are inclined to be unaware of how our inter-subjective realities affect us.

To summarize regarding body and soul:

On one hand, our bodily functions can be sub-conscious.

On the other hand, the institutions of society, entertainment and advertisement branches, social groups, social media and political propaganda affect our psyche in varying degrees and we are, more or less, conscious of its effect on us.

A lack of consciousness about how our society works and of how our bodies work can be detrimental to our psychological well-being.

Our psyche is built to especially focus our attention on things that elicit strong feelings with us. In the context of social media, this increases the probability that we readily share content that pleases us or that evokes fear or feelings of hate within us. Psychological pain related to the body can be derived from all of the dynamics of FRAME-factors.

The brain can reflect on and process sensory input momentarily in a reflexive action but also in a slower more deliberate manner. The uniquely characteristic reaction that each individual manifests is formed by the emotional charge that is reflexively activated in the body in combination with intentional moral considerations that are imposed by enhanced activity within the frontal lobes.

Alluding to Freud, one might say that the "ego" acts as an intermediary between the "superego" which is predominantly situated in the frontal lobes and the more primitive "id" which resides in the basal ganglia.

We are constantly faced with the challenge of reconciling what we subjectively feel and believe (subjective reality), with what is objectively, factually true (objective reality).

There is a risk that we "pull the wool over our own eyes" in an act of self-deception, despite it being obvious to any observing, objective third party that we are being contradictory and hypocritical.

Depending on the situation, due to the relative imbalance in strength between the component elements of the psyche; (using Freud's terminology; the super-ego, the ego and the id), the interaction within the psyche and by extention our behavior may become irrational and inconsistent.

Brunswik´s lense-model can be used as a tool to assess how we transform objective cues into subjective reality.

Using FRAME´S terminology: Formation of external and internal sensory impressions; reactions within the body; reflections of mind; emotions and action, we can analyze the psyche in a different mode and contemplate on whether we achieve our goals or not.

I'm of the opinion that emotional experiences and self-consciousness are objectively dependent on the ability of the brain to form connections between outer and inner phenomena, reflect them and react to resultant hormone levels given the existent corporal neuronal hierarchies that are present in the body.

Psychological pain, in the context of the specific cultural environment we live in, such as feelings of guilt and/or experiences of physical or emotional offence may be due to our having insufficient empathy towards ourselves or others.

Know yourself

History professor, Yuval Harari, notes in his book, "Homo Deus", that the growing number of individuals in the burgeoning towns and kingdoms of the ancient farming communities, led to a relative anonymization of individuals when people could no longer know everyone in their communities.

The introduction of the taxation system in ancient Egypt around 2,500 BC, prompted the development of writing numbers and hieroglyphics as a precursor to the use of the written word.

This was gradually extrapolated into a system of written language which was harnessed to describe and retain the intergenerational narratives that emerged and were passed on, thus consolidating commonly held beliefs and ideas (inter-subjective realities). Accordingly, the prerequisite conditions for hierarchical co-operation on a grand scale with the formation of great armies and religious movements, were guaranteed.

On a personal level, intersubjective realities can vary immensely.

In my work at mental health clinics, I have always found it a rewarding experience to solve the psychological quandaries faced by youths, through creative therapeutic discussion.

A new pedagogical model, FRAMES-model, began to take shape in my mind during therapy sessions.

Given that every client is unique in their own right, I eventually realized, that I could count on the dependability of this model as a solid and reliable psychotherapeutic base (frame of reference).

I found it ideal in the application of the aspects of cognitive behavioral therapy (CBT) along with elements from object relation theory.

In my practice, I used a combination of CBT, gestalt therapy and a theory of relations that I call systemic subject relation theory.

The frame of reference, FRAMES that I outline here has been invaluable for me in my work and I hope that more psychotherapists will discover the advantages it provides.

Allow me to start from the beginning.

Our sensory apparatus i.e. our five extracorporeal senses plus our intracorporeal senses: balance, proprioception and nerve impulses, all send impressions to our brains from the very beginning of life.

Ideally, the dynamic systems of nerve cell activation corresponding to the sensory impressions experienced in the brain of the new-born baby are consolidated in a calm and safe environment.

For example, the child may experience excitement when food is on its way or calm and contentment when it begins to satisfy its hunger.

The infant's sensory apparatus is innately interconnected with the autonomous nervous system allowing sympathetic reflexes (higher pulse due to excitement) and parasympathetic reflexes (lower pulse due to peace and contentment).

Cerebral neuronal activity may be present as a response to the infant's experience of its own and its mother's body, feelings of longing for its mother, stomach ache or other sensory impressions.

The new-born will show its discontent regardless of whether it is due to intracorporeal conditions (hunger, ache etc.) or extracorporeal disturbances (loud noises, cold etc.).

Patterns of recognition of perceived stimuli develop in the brain of the infant and, through repetition, are consolidated as "experience".

The repeated activation of specific neuronal pathways in response to diverse stimuli eventually establish an extensive network of neuronal associations between different visual, linguistic, emotional, memory and executive functions in the brain.

During youth, association pathways that are not reactivated recede. Accordingly, the initial associations that were established in infancy are likely to make the greatest impression on how we interact with others later on in life.

The infant gradually learns to be aware of repetitive patterns that it perceives and subsequent feelings it has when it interacts with its carer, its relation object. (Mother and child are mutually forming an inter-subject reality).

The mother's state of mind is inclined to be mirrored in the child.

Primitive mental reflections gradually start to develop in the sensorimotor activity of the child.

If you shake a little tinker-bell behind a child's ear and the child turns its head to see and hear it, the child shows that it has heard the bell and reacted physically to the sensory stimulus.

Evolutionary requirements have necessitated that infants are born with a grasp reflex in order to hold on to their mother.

However, the child has to learn to inhibit the grasp reflex in order to refine the motor co-ordination in its hand so that it can learn to examine, grasp and let go of objects.

Gradually, voluntary motor function and focused attention develop.

The Swiss psychologist Jean Piaget has described how primal mental reflection is shaped during the sensorimotor development of each individual.

The English cognitive researcher, Anil Seth, has concluded that consciousness is created through systemic communication i.e. from the body to the brain (bottom-up) and conversely from the brain to the body, inner organs, musculoskeletal system and the sensory apparatus (top down).

The brain receives and transmits nerve-signals to and from the rest of the body. This dynamic neural pathway communication forms consciousness.

Anil Seth describes three dimensional aspects to consciousness:

Consciousness on a scale from unconscious to awake, the substance of consciousness and conscious awareness of oneself.

All of these dimensions are essential in our experience of being. There is a minimal threshold level of consciousness required in order to fire up the action of neural pathways to accommodate perception, action, emotions and mental reflection.

Self-awareness matures when the ability to reflect on experiences grows.

Reoccurring events lead to specific patterns of association in the brain. To put it one way, the autonomous nervous system, responsible for the reflexes of fight or flight, freezing or being calm, creates expectations about what we are about to feel, see and hear.

Expectations about those experiences will focus our concentration of attention.

Our comprehension and selective attention are used to forecast the most predictable scenario that might be expected based on previously learned information and situations.

Intuition leads to certain thoughts and associated emotions, creating either positive or negative expectations depending on the bodily reactions that are generated by that intuition.

If an event generates stressing bodily reactions that previously caused worrying thoughts, similar events may in turn lead to the same apprehension.

As we grow up apprehension or the lure of satisfaction play major roles in our lives.

We can challenge our apprehensions by acting in new ways and noticing the consequences this new behavior brings to our experiences. If we succeed with this in some aspired activity or behavior then that new characteristic can satisfactorily be consolidated in our brains make-up.

As we grow, we learn to read between the lines (seeing beyond the obvious) to develop our ability to think abstractly. Our ability to comprehend nuances and draw better measured conclusions increases. Accordingly, the older we get, the better our ability to make good decisions. Our cognitive capacity increases.

When I started my research studies at the Institute of Psychology at Umeå University all the professors were researching the decision-making processes using Brunswiks Lense model.

Brunswiks theoretical model explains the relationship between objective phenomena (cues) and decisions made based on those cues. A major weakness in our research was that the parameters used did not include those of "satisfaction" or "inner stress".

However, we reasoned that experimental research in psychology should be based on "theories of small or middle-range" that can be extrapolated to arrive at more overarching theoretical models about the human psyche.

For family reasons, we moved from Umeå and I never got the chance to complete my research studies.

However, there was one example about deductive reasoning that stood out in my mind.

Consider a nurse taking calls from patients and trying to assess the reason for three symptoms: headache, fever and general body pain.

There are many different causes of headache. Fever could be the body's reaction to something, but what could that be? Pain all over could also be caused by many different factors.

The nurse's experience will help her assess the probability that the symptoms are a result of different underlying conditions.

When she establishes that the caller has no other symptoms than these three, she can use factor analysis thinking to assess the probability of whether the patient has the flu or some other illness.

Brunswiks Lense model illustrates not only the probability of a correlation between a phenomenon and an objective reality but also people's conclusions about the probable cause of what they experience.

In other words, the Brunswiks Lense model allows us to see the relationship between probability assessments we derive from subjective contra objective reality.

The Lense model and factor analysis probability theory subsequently came to influence me in my counselling work at a mental health clinic for youths.

I tried to determine the underlying psychology of my clients based on the manner in which they recounted their problems and what mental reflections they made.

As a result, I devised a psychological framework model, a mind-map for assessment of dynamic experiences.

Sometimes I saw the framework model as a picture in my mind, sometimes I used the whiteboard to map-out the different aspects of the problem during sessions.

It is common knowledge that we have five senses: sight, hearing, smell, taste and touch.

However, we also have the inner senses that relay impulses from the body to the brain such as proprioception and balance that communicate experiences of movement and dance but even of tension and uncertainty.

Other neural pathways signal when we are hungry or full, need to relieve ourselves, have a pain, are stressed, have palpitations etc. etc.

These are all signals to the brain from our inner organs, skin, muscles and fasciae and provide information about our body's status.

Sight gives us the perception of color and shape. Hearing allows us to experience sound, song, words and sentences.

The senses of taste and smell in combination with stimuli to pressure and heat sensitive receptors in the mouth and jaws allow us to experience the aroma, flavor, consistency and temperature of the food we eat.

The skins receptors allow us to experience heat, touch and the embrace of a loved one.

The body has a two-way system of neural pathways leading signals from the body into the brain and reciprocally from the brain out to maintain bodily functions.

An example of this is the Reticular activating system (RAS) which is a network of neurons located in the brain stem at its intersection with the spinal cord. This area acts as a juncture for neural signals, from the body, on their way up from the spinal cord to the brain and conversely for neural signals sent from the brain down to the spinal cord from where they are ultimately transmitted to their relevant focus points in the body.

The South African psychoanalyst and neuro-psychologist, Mark Solms, has shown the importance of RAS for us as acting subjects, in monitoring our emotions and our self-consciousness.

The interaction between our senses and our brains is a pre-requisite for the ability to experience ourselves as separate entities and give us a sense of context in the surrounding world. Our sensory make-up and brains allow us to experience what it is to exist.

Although my research studies had been curtailed, they had elicited my avid interest and fascination with the crucial role that the sensory apparatus has in our psychological functioning.

Researchers with access to functional brain-scanning equipment and who assess external and internal sensory impressions, bodily conditions, actions, thoughts and emotions have the perfect opportunity to research the dynamics of consciousness within a scientific framework for deriving theoretical content.

The years that I've spent as a licensed psychologist in sessions with teenagers and young adults, using applied psychology, can be seen as my own personal journey in research.

Apart from being biological beings in our own right, we also have an active role as participants in the diverse social contexts that we experience.

Gradually, the work that materialized on the whiteboard I used during sessions with my clients, allowed me to create the summarized psychological overview seen below. This overview has given me an insight into how we function bio-psycho-socially.

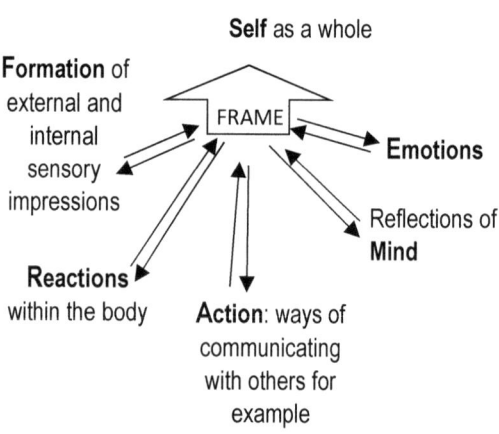

Within psychodynamics, variable FRAME-functions interact with each other leading to a variety of ways of perceiving ourselves as persons in various contexts.

In my first book from 2004, I introduced a new psychodynamic model, "FRAME:S A psychological frame of reference". The capital letter S was meant to signify oneself as a whole.

The acronym FRAMES can also be seen as the plural form of FRAME.

You might say that a person's inner identity gradually becomes a potpourri of many FRAMES.

Everything has an effect on the brain and when the dynamics in our overall experiences have settled, an inner identity is formed of all our selfper-ceptions.

The abbreviation of the models name came from combining the constituent letters in a way that made it easy for me to see the big picture, as I reflected on my client's story.

During sessions I chose words that would guide the conversation so that analysis could be made using FRAMES. Examples of some good questions are: What do you notice? How does your body react? What do you do then? What thoughts do you have when that happens? What feelings do you experience? What consequences do you anticipate?

Our senses allow us to experience our environment and what happens within our bodies. Our internal organs regulate physiological balance and well-being. Life forces us to act. We think which in turn elicits emotional reactions.

Psychological development is an on-going process. New experiences are acquired and added to the multiple experiences we've already had in an ever-growing catalogue of experiences we store in our brains. New connections in the brain lead to new associations.

Connections in the brain can integrate our ability to recognize patterns in what we are currently experiencing and associate them with experiences that we have had in the past i.e. aha moments or sudden insights.

New sensory impressions are associated to memories as earlier patterns of synapse activation are recognized and reconsolidated.

As we sleep impressions and reflections we have had during the day are processed and restructured.

How do we form concepts about the future and how it will be? How are desire and dreams about the future shaped?

Gradually, personal plans and aspirations can be formed as new behavior is put in relation to how we thought and acted in similar situations in the past.

All the FRAME-factors are interconnected in one way or another.

Mental pictures can be related to physical activity.

Hearing a song can trigger certain emotions.

Different aromas can bring early memories and feelings to mind.

Emotions inspire actions.

The mental associations we have in our minds can cause distress or relaxation.

A long list can be made of the systemic connections between the FRAMES-factors.

In time, the individual's ability for reflection develops as the brain integrates networks of neurons from the sensory system, the musculoskeletal system and networks in the auto-nomous nervous system.

I take for granted that future research of psychological perspectives will be strongly linked to neurophysiological research of consciousness. Psychological development involves integration of previous experiences with newly made experiences.

In our minds, we can live in the past, the present or have dreams about the future. This gives us the opportunity to live fulfilling lives as it inspires exploration and discovery.

All biological, psychological and sociological systems provide feed-back mechanisms.

The following summary shows the psychological feedback mechanisms between how we perceive ourselves and mental reflection.

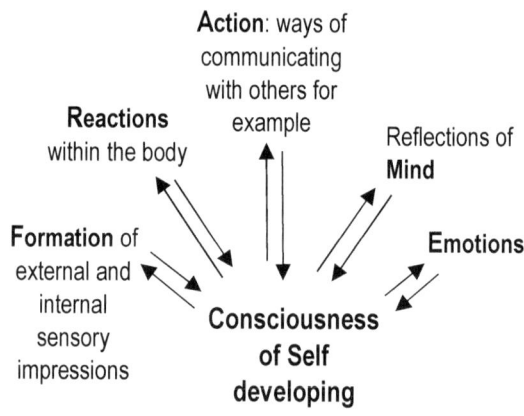

There is a concurrent evolution of consciousness of self and consciousness of social networks that the individual is a part of.

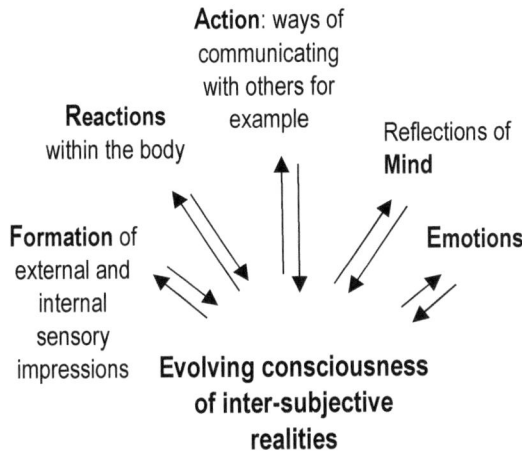

Advances in mental development and experience lead to the growth of integrity and maturity.

On a societal level our ideologies are intertwined with the nature of our material world.

In order to develop society, we have to try to understand how it functions, given the clash between social and economic interests.

My view is that in order to develop psychologically we cannot underestimate the role that our selectively biased perception plays in influencing our thoughts, feelings and actions.

Selectively biased perception can entail negligence of background information or ignoring alternative information. It can impede our cognitive ability and is responsible for many break-downs in communication. This selectivity creates a blind spot in our self-perception and impedes perception of the world around us.

Selectivity can come from limiting individual perspective and adhering to group think, which hinders psychological and societal development.

In Freud's era, society was still heavily influenced by the teachings of the bible. The Old Testaments story about Adam and Eve being tempted by the serpent in the Garden of Eden (Paradise) was used as a parable to discourage sexual relations outside of marriage. Accordingly, sex and sexuality became a greatly charged subject, a taboo for men and women alike.

Selectively biased perception under the imposition of these moral codes caused problems, not only on a psychological plane, where sexual urges were laden with guilt and shame, but even on a sociological level with polarization of women as being either depraved or holy.

The cognitive researcher, Anil Seth sub-divides the concept of "consciousness of self" into five categories: bodily self, perspectival self, volitional self, narrative self and social self.

When I saw his lecture, from the The Royal Institution in London, on YouTube, I was struck by the similarities between the five FRAMES-factors and his five aspects of the "self".

Even if the parameters of the "self" are not described by Anil Seth in exactly the same way as the FRAMES-parameters, their overall similarities make them relatable to each other:

"Bodily self": *Reactions* within the body, inner organs, musculoskeletal system, the sensory apparatus, the central nervous system and the autonomic nervous system i.e. psychosomatic function.

In my counselling sessions at the youth health center, I usually concentrated on my client's focus of attention, stress reflexes and mind-traps.

Some of my clients were worried about their appearance. They perceived themselves differently depending on the attire they had or the make-up they used.

I have noticed how my perception of my own reflection in the mirror changes depending on what mood I'm in. Therefore, I believe that attention to one's appearance is a perceptible factor in self-consciousness.

"Perspectival self": *Formation* of external and internal sensory impressions.

"Volitional self": *Emotions*, that govern our volitional life.

"Narrative self": Reflections of *Mind* and our life story.

"Social self": *Action* including how we and others apprehend our social behavior.

A common quandary that psychotherapists have to tackle is whether to focus on the client's present circumstances and how to deal with them or to address the issue of sensitive personal relationships with parents and other influential people.

My view is that the therapy process should involve both current issues and things that have happened in the past, i.e., how fear, worry, anger or prolonged periods of poor mental health were handled.

We are continually navigating the times we live in and how society around us functions.

In a world of rapid information flow, spiritual mindfulness has become an ideal tool to counter the myriad of information and sensory stimuli that we are bombarded with in our hectic, modern lifestyles.

I've used the enforced isolation during the Corona pandemic to become more mindful, gather my thoughts, reflect and write about the two psychological schools of thought, object relation theory and behaviorism and how the FRAMES model can bridge the gap between these traditional viewpoints.

Human interaction

To provide my clients with an understanding of psychology and instill in them a sense of co-herence, I needed a tool for psychoeducation and a simple mind-map to illustrate the entire gamut of psychological make-up.

Gestalt therapy role-play can be used to activate experiences of self that clients want to analyze. However, during sessions, I also needed a theoretical frame of reference to help me and my clients reflect on our psychological reality.

Cognitive behavioral therapy uses the formula S-R-C, where S stands for stimulus, R for response and C for consequence.

Another concept within CBT is that of S-O-R-C with S denoting stimulus, O organism, R response and C denoting the consequences of a particular re-sponse.

However, in therapy sessions with my clients, I felt that I needed a method to include the important part of the psychological jigsaw puzzle, *focus of attention*.

As a psychology student, I gained insight into the Brunswik Lense model that provides a window between objective and subjective context. It allows us to see the relationship between sensory impressions and how we interpret what we perceive. It makes clear that what a client regards as a stimulus (trigger to a response) doesn't necessarily equate to what the therapist sees as a trigger.

The FRAMES-model can illustrate how a certain episode, for example, someone in the family sighing, may be interpreted by one person as irritation while another sibling might only see the sigh as a sign of relaxation.

Objectively, a sigh might be the result of irritation but it could even be an attempt to be less irritated.

Each individual interprets the sigh based on his/her own particular set of thoughts and feelings. Given that each individual has their own unique thoughts and feelings, their interpretations can lead to different conclusions and thereby different subjective realities.

For example, it is not obvious that the therapist and the client will share the same analysis of what bodily reactions and worries may result from a high-school student being abandoned by their best friend from middle-school.

In order to improve my psychoanalysis, I wanted to incorporate Brunswiks view of the relationship between outer and spiritual phenomena and their underlying causes.

If we are blinded by our own biases, or our own strong feelings are allowed to cloud our judgement then we will be likely to think and act in a predictable, preconditioned way. Our interpretation of the situation may mislead us and misguide our subsequent focus of attention.

Selectively directed attention can trap us in a subjective reality limiting our understanding of the psychodynamic facets operating within us and the sociological dynamics in our lives.

In a relationship between two individuals who crave attention and approval, if one of them feels that the other doesn't appreciate or respect their feelings or opinions, then the relationship will rest on shaky grounds.

In my therapeutic practice, I wanted reactions in the autonomous nervous system to be a criterion in my analysis of anxiety.

We discussed the role of physical sensations as a fundamental mediator of trepidation and anxiety and how physical reactions to stress can further overexert the body during a panic attack.

Attention focus affects how panic attacks develop.

Stress elicits physical reactions (stress reflexes) in the form of fight or flight or may even cause the individual to freeze. In certain social situations, these reactions may be triggered and cause tunnel vision, where what we hear and see is selectively honed in on the perceived threat, leading to a flustered and agitated state.

If the situation worsens and the physical reactions to this stress are allowed to escalate a panic attack may ensue.

The simultaneous activity (outward bound/inward bound signals) in pathways between the brain and the body when anxiety is present, can lead to erratic, fleeting perceptual focus, confusion and stress reflexes thereby heightening the panic.

Individuals who experience panic attacks can be totally caught off guard.

The individual afflicted by a panic attack, may well have been aware of mounting inner-stress but it is only when stress reflexes cause heart palpitations to become so manifest and breathing frequency so elevated that hyperventilation and shortness of breath are apparent, that the sheer shock of the panic attack is felt.

An example of when such a sequence of events can occur is when people find themselves in an argument with someone who means a lot to them and emotions are running high.

During sessions, I was guided by the vernacular of my clients. Accordingly, I preferred to use words like action and reaction instead of words like behavior and response.

Subsequently, I decided to use the abbreviation "FRAME" as the name of my model, given that that word was formed from the capital letters in the five variable psychological functions that I chose to represent a holistic view of the dynamic psychology of humans.

The holistic nature of experiencing relationships includes formation of sensory impressions (F), physical reactions (R), actions (A) towards the object of one´s feelings, mental reflections (M) and emotions.

The ability to handle ambivalence increases by developing so-called object permanence in relation to external and internal objects. Please see final chapter (You and me).

The shaping of the active individuals external persona in relation to the other, is all about how the other individual experiences the one who is active (subject). The active person's inner identity is dependent on how the subject perceives himself as the acting agent in the relationship.

If you want to analyze the psychological dynamics at play in your psyche you can start with the F-factor in FRAMES (formation of sensory impressions), then reflect on how the F-factor interacts with physical reactions (R-factor), actions (A-factor), mental reflections (M-factor) and emotions (E-factor).

As FRAMES is a dynamic psychological framework model you can use any of the factors from which to initiate the psychological analysis of yourself and the events that befall you.

Psychological factor analysis allows us to reflect on how the disparate psychological variables interact with self-perception and if one factor stands out as an explanation for one's own behavior.

The inner persona might be built specifically on notions about our interactions with loved-ones but even on memories and reflections of how we interacted with objects of hate.

We are most influenced by people who elicit strong feelings and lively reflections within us.

During my long career as a psychologist, I have sometimes noticed a certain animosity between object relation theorists and CBT-therapists.

When I decided to write this book about psycho-therapeutic theories, in order to bridge the gap between CBT and the psychodynamic view-point using object relation theory, it was because these opposing viewpoints are merely theoretical and yet they are responsible for a lot of conflict within the healthcare sector.

A lot of psychologists already employ integrated elements from both the object relation theory and cognitive behavioral science but, like me, they may lack a theoretical frame of reference to alleviate integration of these two fields of psychotherapy.

In my opinion, the advantage of a client-focused, psychodynamic work model, is that it makes it easy for the therapist to adapt treatment to suit the client's process.

Every client is unique. Some clients prefer a structured work model including home assignments whereas others are more at ease with work with models where the client acts-out spontaneously with the help of the therapist.

In my work with youths, it was important for me to adjust my treatment to suit my clients and I noticed that many youths were incapable of completing their home assignments.

However, breathing exercises that they mastered in the clinical setting (see the chapter about

FRAMES-analysis) often proved to be easy to remember and perform at home.

In daily life, attention is focused on different events. Good breathing technique requires regular practice and can easily be neglected. It is important to bring it back into focus and maintain it routinely.

Hopefully, observing good breathing technique can help to alleviate nervous tension when anxiety builds during stressful situations at home or in school.

There are many aspects characterizing family culture: atmosphere, openness, method of communication, how love is shown, intimacy (distancing between family members), hierarchical or democratic culture, rigid or dynamic reasoning and acting, taking responsibility and so on.

Interaction may entail the establishment of clear or ambiguous personal boundaries (read the chapter "You and me").

The atmosphere in a school-class or at a workplace affects individuals similarly and can be described using the same parameters.

Relationships can be both nurturing and destructive.

All of us, irrespective of whether we are object or subject, have built in reflexes for the situations we experience in life. Our awareness of these may vary but a few examples that virtually everyone has experienced are the fight or flight reflex, the freeze response or the sensation of being calm.

To be part of a mutual, subject relation we must share our inner desires, thoughts and feelings with each other.

When a relationship is functioning well each individual finds it easier to accommodate an adequate inner object, even if the object is not physically present.

According to object relation theory, a person who can grasp that an object relation can be experienced as both nurturing and attritional, can experience object permanence.

If we integrate the FRAMES-model in an object relations analysis and highlight both the objects and the subject's experiences, we can describe and analyze an object relation as seen in the matrix below.

The Subjects and the Objects respective FRAMES:

	The subjects experience of the relationship	The objects experience of the relationship
FRAMES of the subject and the object respektively	The subjects consciousness of self in their inter-subjective reality	The objects consciousness of self in their inter-subjective reality
Respektive FRAMES as they reflect on the past	The subjects memories of the interaction	The objects memories of the interaction
Respektive FRAMES as they reflect on the future	The subjects expectations of the inter-action	The subjects expectations of the inter-action

Every relationship has its low points, whether they are healthy or unhealthy. Relationships involve an acting subject, who interacts in dynamic engagements where external and internal requirements vary in those involved.

Interaction is the essence of a relationship. Both partners think about the relationship, both have feelings for each other, both experience themselves as a separate and independent ego in the relationship.

The matrix on the previous page is unilateral. Accordingly, it should be mirrored so that the object can also be visualized as the subject.

This illustrates the complexity of subject relationships. In one analysis, one of the individuals is seen as object while the other individual can also be seen as object in a juxtaposed, mirrored analysis.

This reciprocal nature of subject relations can make judgements about possible outcomes hard to predict whether the analysis is of object or subject, relationships, groups, families or society at large.

The more self-aware we are, the more in-tune we are with our feelings and desires and the greater our knowledge about socio-psychological and sociological situations, the easier it will be to gauge how life pans out.

As we go through life we are influenced by the dynamics in our family, the company we keep in school and in our spare time, our relationships at work and so on.

Important relationships for youths are those they have in real life (IRL), through interactions on the internet and the internal relationships they have within themselves.

What are the dynamics of idolatry? Is there a reciprocal nature to the communication between idols and their worshipers?

Common objectives and projects fortify relationships. In the beginning of a relationship, it is easier to come up with exciting projects if you involve all relevant parties in the process.

One young woman I had, in therapy with her reluctant partner, later, in private, told me about an episode she had experienced in the pub.

The couple had overheard a quarrel between another young couple which prompted her boyfriend to suggest that they contact the youth clinic about counselling.

Sometimes, I'm struck by the realization that people should go in relationship therapy, when they are still young and in-love, not just wait until they are about to break-up. Thus, they could focus on each other's expectations of their partner, instead of having to hash out their disappointment with each other when the relationship is on the rocks.

The disappointments may simply be a result of neglecting to clearly stipulate the expectations each had on one another from the beginning.

In relationships, feelings of abandonment and betrayal can lie deep in a person's psyche.

Emotional reactions the young child has to events, such as utter yearning for someone dear, may come to light, as the child's experience of life and the world around it develops.

According to object relation theorists the formation of an inner ego can start very early in a child's development. Ideally, the child's behavior will have plenty of good objects to relate to.

Later on in life, if therapy is needed, the therapist can help the client to recall and experience formative feelings of abandonment in their background story.

This makes it possible, in the present, to process feelings related to past experiences.

Working through object relations increases the chance of realizing that inner object formation, mirrors our own feelings towards the object.

The FRAMES-dynamic allows us to create the relation object within ourselves. Object relations are shaped through interaction with those individuals who are the object of our feelings.

An inner shape forms in our minds. Since we are the ones who shape our own object formations, then we are also the ones who can rebuild and adjust our inner conceptions so that we can finally move on.

For our own sakes, if we forgive someone for breaking our confidence, we should not do so, gullibly.

One of the most important factors necessary to give someone trust, is a confidence in our own ability to manage anything that might be thrown at us.

We need to see every individual, every emotional object, as a unique individual with self-awareness and understand that every relationship involves two equal parties.

Selectively directed negative attention may be heightened by an anticipation of conflict and negative emotions.

Selectively directed positive attention may be heightened when we are subject to infatuation. When the "feel-good hormone", oxytocin is coursing through our veins, we tend to notice the positive traits in the object of our passion.

It is virtually impossible to discern, individually, all the conceivable sensory stimuli that exist.

Partly because we almost exclusively focus our attention only on that which attracts us.

There are clear limits to the number of stimuli that our external and internal senses can register.

One advantage of Gestalt therapy is that it encourages the use of as many senses as possible during therapy. Sense of movement, visual and auditory sensory impressions are used to work through whatever issues the client has. Theoretically, even smell and taste can be used in the sessions.

It can be cathartic to reflect on painful memories with a therapist who can reactivate, receive and understand our traumatic experiences, including failed attempts at bonding with others.

This makes it possible to recall and work through deeply anchored inner experiences, stamped in our consciousness by traumatic events.

Conceptions formed as a result of our reaction to previously traumatizing inner objects can then be brought to light so that they no longer hamper our interactions with others in the present.

We can come to the realization that it's possible for us to act in a more open/spontaneous manner, that inner objects created old conceptions that are no longer relevant.

They may have become irrelevant because the object is no longer a part of our external reality or we may have practiced to change our mind's focus to avoid automatically invoking nefarious conceptions.

My mentor in gestalt therapy illustrated in a surprisingly easy way how the perception of a person could be colored by the memories they had of their interactions with people in the past.

During therapeutic role-play when I had an imaginary dialogue with a person who was currently a part of my life, my mentor interjected and asked if I was simultaneously having a dialogue with another relation gestalt in my life.

It became immediately apparent to me that this was, in fact, the case. I also instantly knew exactly who that person was.

I was then instructed to have an imaginary dialogue with the disturbing character from the past wherein I voiced not only my own thoughts but also the imaginary replies that I expected from the other party in that interaction.

This was confirmation that this was all taking place at that given moment, within my own mind.

On my way home from mentoring, I felt a catharsis, a release from the disturbance the former character had exerted over me.

I could break free from earlier conceptions, allowing me to engage in genuine and honest dialogue with the person who I was currently interacting with.

If another person treats us in a mind-boggling way, it may be the result of our own incorporation of a past, object relation in the current interaction or that the other person himself is affected by past associations.

It becomes more incomprehensible if both parties' perceptions are clouded by their own inner object conceptions as that means that, at least four conceptions are present despite there being only two individuals involved.

It can get even more confusing in conflicts involving group relations as even more inner conceptions are involved due to every single one of the group members, having their own individual inner objects and conceptions from the past.

Therapeutical relationship

The relationship between client and therapist is a special one in several ways. The client seeks help in handling life's problems and is ready to talk about things that can be embarrassing or shameful such as feelings of insecurity, anxiety and depression.

The youths I met had come to the realization that their well-being was so impacted that they wanted the guidance of a therapist to reflect on their circumstances.

A client must have come to the insight that they need for psychotherapy in order to understand and accept their problem. They must see the role of psychotherapy in reaching self-awareness.

If therapy is to succeed, it is crucial for the client to actively want to and be able to reflect on their feelings, thoughts and actions.

Care and concern shown for people who are in therapy may be soothing but the primary goal of psychotherapeutic intervention is to give the client a conscious awareness of the role of feelings, perceptions and thoughts in their own behavior and their subsequent consequences. It gives the client the tools to take responsibility for themselves as bio-psycho-social beings.

A therapeutic relationship is just as susceptible to and affected by biased attention and associated feelings. A clients' inability to trust a therapist might be due the therapist reminding the client of some negative object in their life.

Accordingly, the client may behave dismissively towards the therapist when some sensitive issue is brought up. In response, the therapist may react negatively and the therapeutical flow and creativity between therapist and client may be compromised.

One might assume that a psychotherapist who has a keen ear and is very attentive could nonetheless be successful in the role as therapist despite the difficult situation. However, body language can transmit strong signals of rejection which even the accomplished therapist might subconsciously mirror in their own body-language without even realizing it.

In such a scenario, the therapist needs to take responsibility for acknowledging the problem and in co-operation with the client devise a method to facilitate progression in their discussions.

If they are successful, it could be an eye-opener for the client to see that it was possible to discuss such a sensitive issue with the therapist.

I applied a behavioristic and gestalt therapeutic method in my practice, sometimes employing the use of exercises that had to be reflected on until the next session.

In the back of my mind, I had the object relation theory mindset. Did I remind my client of someone else in their life?

In other words, could our discourse be affected by negative associations the client had regarding some inner object gestalt in their life?

Could it provoke a reciprocal tide of unresolved emotions within myself, festering feelings I had for someone earlier on in my life? If so, how would it affect the therapeutic process in session?

I usually felt that my clients associated some good inner object relation to our therapy sessions which allowed us both to feel comfortable and safe.

Due to the inequality in status within the therapeutical relationship, the onus to create the right atmosphere for an open dialogue always falls on the therapist.

A therapist who finds himself overwhelmed by connotations of negative emotions, should seek guidance from their mentor or maybe even consider referring the client to another therapist.

A therapist may feel overwhelmed due to the shocking and unfathomable nature of the client's story which may make it too hard to take on the role of therapist.

If serious psychiatric disturbances are present the therapist can be subjected to even more demanding and trying circumstances. For some examples, please see "Leva nu" or "Relation före metod" in the reference section.

In my therapy work with youths, behavioristic concepts, based on Pavlov's and Skinner's research with animal subjects, using terms such as stimulus and response led to my thinking about human behavior and relationships, in an objectifying, from the outside looking in, perspective.

This irked me when I started working with the young people who came seeking guidance.

I wanted to help the youths to understand themselves within the parameters of their own subjective description of their anxiety.

It was important to incorporate language that wasn´t construed as distancing. I wanted to acknowledge their subjective experiences and ensure a good working environment for me and my young clients.

Additionally, my young clients needed to gain elementary, objective information about the physiology of anxiety and sometimes even be presented with a sociological research perspective in order to facilitate a good working environment based on a scientific frame of reference.

The youths needed information about the physiological and psychological processes that cause anxiety i.e. the body's' autonomic nervous system and psychosocial factors that contribute to anxiety.

They needed to find a way to understand their own actions and thoughts.

I initiated every series of therapy sessions by asking my client what they needed help with.

Allowing the young clients to put into their own words what they needed help with gave me insight into their patterns of thought about their problems.

The first step in successful therapy is to establish a sense of trust and mutual co-operation towards a common goal.

I could gauge my young clients' attitude to our communication by their answers to my opening questions.

Quite often, my client started the session by stating that "I don't know where to begin"

Lately, I have started sessions by asking if I can sketch out a FRAME-structure to illustrate the problem or if my client wants to begin by openly and subjectively associating to open questions.

In the 1970's, linguists Richard Bandler and John Grinder, made behavioral observations of renowned psychotherapists and attempted to understand the mechanisms behind their effective communication with their clients. They concluded the following:

Successful therapists had an inherent ability to intuit and adjust their behavior to the dominant mood that was apparent in their clients' choice of words.

Clients whose communication was predominantly characterized by the visual could use such expressions as "I can't see any solution to my problem".

Clients whose dominant sensory channel was auditive used expressions such as "no-one seems to listen to what I have to say".

More proprioceptively influenced clients could describe their situation as "feeling weighed down".

I noticed that my clients could have some particular one of the FRAME-functions to the fore at the beginning of the therapy sessions.

Some might focus on their actions in a certain situation. Others could focus on how a family member had acted. Other clients might start off by describing their feelings. Some were preoccupied by worry. Still others recounted their bodily symptoms.

Both my client and I could influence the direction the session could take. If I suggested a certain exercise, for example an imaginary dialogue between my client and someone in his circles, I always assured myself that my client was ok with it.

Tone of voice, facial expressions, body-language and the spoken word are all important in therapy sessions.

However, these same factors can also hamper sessions as they can bring to mind some triggering object in the clients lived experience.

At the end of every session, I asked if we should meet again. Accordingly, I could ascertain whether or not the client felt that we were on the right track. A positive response reinforced our commitment to our work-relationship.

Anxiety

A young man with compulsive syndrome trains at the gym every single day to bulk up his musculature. After a friend notices the compulsive nature of his training, he comments:

I just have to make sure I get to the gym and train.

His friend: Don't you ever rest?

The young man with compulsive behavior feels anxious by not being seen as "normal" and as a result he lies that he didn't train yesterday despite him actually having trained a full pass then.

His friend doesn't believe him but keeps quiet.

The only person who really knows the truth is the young compulsively neurotic man. His anxiety level is often so high and his behavior so compulsive and automatic that he actually finds it hard to remember if he exercised yesterday.

His problem with anxiety leads to problems not only for himself but even for his friend as it causes doubt about the honesty in their conversation and, by extension, in their relationship.

The problem is that they are not being open about the young mans' compulsive training being fueled by an underlying anxiety.

The lower anxiety level is present only as long as he feels that he has trained just a short time ago or if he feels calmer for some other reason. This calmness is present only as long as no other stressful circumstances or thoughts surface and lead to brooding.

Anxiety is rooted in the reaction of the body's' sympathetic nervous system.

Leaving aside the relational problem between these two friends, let us concentrate on the young mans, more or less, constant anxious state.

What is anxiety?

Being worried is a sign that there is a state of alert present in the brain that is reflexively preparing for fight, paralysis or flight. The levels of stress hormones in the body become elevated.

My experience as a primary healthcare psychotherapist is that a large portion of my clients have a tense costal breathing pattern (activating the sympathetic nervous system) with a subsequent risk of feelings of distress in everyday life: frustration, agitation, irritability, bitterness, reluctance, forced happiness, fear, shame and so on.

Constricted, superficial costal breathing can mask chronic hyperventilation (respiratory alkalosis with compenasatory physiological reactions) that is harmful for both physical and psychological well-being and increases the risk for feelings of panic.

In the 70's psychotherapists who utilized object relations theory conceded that cognitive behaviorists might well help their patients overcome phobias and compulsive behavior but they could not help them address their deeper existential angst.

Freud encouraged his patients to openly associate about their problems.

Using Freud's frame of reference to analyze their reflections, the patients could then be aware of their own psychological processes and find an explanation for their anxiety, i.e. conflicts between the id, the ego and the superego.

Modern day sexuality is not laden with shame in the same way as in Freud's era and we must therefore try to find an explanation for feelings of guilt and shame in a broader light (refer to "Från skuld till självrespekt" in the list of references).

Feelings of guilt based on the individual's perception of themselves can vary in depth depending on how encompassing those feelings were during their childhood development and they can become fundamental for the individuals' level of self-esteem.

Pavlov's experimental results from situationally learned physiological reflexes and Skinner´s experiment with instrumental (goal-oriented) conditioning, gave us two new schools within psychology.

The object-relation theoretical school with roots in Freud's practice and the conditioned learning psychological school of Pavlov's and Skinner´s research gave us two main branches within psychotherapy with separate interpretations of anxiety.

Object-relation theory: The client has faced so offensive or chaotic feelings in their relationships that they have difficulty in managing them.

The client needs to feel that their relationship traumas can be brought up and discussed openly. What they then bring up can shape healthy feelings in their relationships.

Optimally the client then feels that their thoughts and expressed feelings can be communicated to a competent therapist who can help them reflect and understand their problems.

Conditioned-learning psychology: Anxiety is generated by automatic thoughts that are formed by physiological reflexes, cognitive dissonance and focus of attention.

These two branches of psychotherapy along with humanistic, client-focused therapy, family therapy and environmental therapy have all been prominent during the 20th century offering different approaches to treatment.

As a newly graduated psychologist I was indoctrinated in the vein of the behavioristic mind-set but later as my experience accumulated, I also became influenced by and incorporated other treatment options into my treatment sessions such as the active values method, object relation theoretical and gestalt therapeutical methods.

I found myself conflicted around these different psychological branches.

As luck would have it, my work at the Youth clinic gave me the opportunity to find a solution to my dilemma.

I became aware that the different lines of approach within the two schools of thought created a cognitive dissonance within me. One had the perspective from within our psyche (object-relation theory, humanistic psychology and gestalt therapy) whilst the other adopted an externally observational approach (behavioral therapy).

The insight that solved my theoretical dilemma was gained from several sources:

Piaget and his theories on conceptual learning.

Behavioral analysis in Cognitive behavioral therapy (CBT) that emphasizes the consequences of situationally-learned thoughts, feelings and behavior.

The Brunswik lense model with its theoretical base that gives insight into the relationship between what we focus our attention on and the consequent conclusions we draw.

Gestalt therapeutical role-play which provides a vehicle for dialogue with ourselves and important figures in our lives.

My time working as a family therapist at a child-psychiatric clinic led to family-system interpretations predominating my thought process.

However, the decisive puzzle-bit that finally solved my theoretical conundrum, was to apply the enlightening, psychological concept of stimulus to each individuals unique perception. This facilitated my awareness of the subjective and selective aspects of my client's experience of the various scenarios they were subjected to.

Accordingly, I never had to concern myself about whether my clients' story was true or false, objectively speaking.

The perceptions of people are influenced by their level of stress, their thoughts, feelings and habits.

Things can be subjectively true while in fact objectively false.

When a client wants to work through their feelings towards a contentious person in their life but put aside their own role in the context i.e., disregard their own psychodynamic process, the therapist may need to help the client understand that both parties' feelings and thoughts are interlinked with their own individual selective attentions.

Psychotherapy is intent on discovering both objective and subjective truths in order to be as honest and genuine as possible with ourselves and others (refer to "Adjustment of mental reflections" page 111).

The fact that perception and cognition are not really the same thing became apparent to me when I did my research within the Brunswik lense model.

Perception and attention are not the same thing. Attention is more associated with vigilance, being on one's guard.

Sleeping difficulties associated with psychological crises, can be explained by the integral relationship between alertness and insomnia.

Statistic factor analysis, the method used in our research on cognitive processes, was also in the back of my mind when I was looking for an effective treatment mode with my young patients.

Psychological factor analysis can be described as reflecting on how one reacts, feels and acts in different situations.

Based on my own life and career experience, I understood that selectively focused attention, corporal reactions, thoughts and emotions could explain why we behave the way we do.

Stress reflexes and focused attention are important parameters for insomnia which was a common reason for school personnel and/or parents seeking help at the Youth clinic.

Quite commonly, school curators or parents would urge their charges to seek me out at the Youth Health Center, mostly because they were worried about the child's sleeping difficulties.

We always made sure that the youths themselves actually wanted to meet me for therapy.

The young patients might have found themselves experiencing dizziness, palpitations and felt like they were being suffocated, not understanding the psychosomatic mechanisms behind these symptoms, especially if it was their first time experiencing a panic attack.

The presenting youths commonly did not know much about fight- or flight reflexes or becoming frozen in fear. They weren't aware that these reactions could explain the resultant tense muscle tonus, palpitations and raised breathing frequency, which in extreme cases could lead to hyperventilation and panic.

Hyperventilation causes precisely those symptoms that my patients with panic and anxiety recounted, albeit in varying, individual manifestations. Many of them had sleeping problems. Some had even fainted during a panic-attack.

Many didn´t realize that their anticipatory anxiety originated in their fear of becoming anxious again, in a similar situation to that which triggered their first anxiety attack.

In sessions I taught them about good breathing pattern in which the belly protrudes naturally during relaxed inhalation and passively retracts in exhalation. They were able to practice relaxed breathing which worked wonders for them psychologically.

Clients could then use what they had learned about focusing on correct diaphragm breathing, in everyday life.

Many were so elated with the result that this insight gave them that they no longer needed more help.

However, in everyday life it is easy to lose sight of newly acquired skills and this enables panic to be constant threat.

Therefore, it may be necessary to rekindle the insights learned, by engaging in subsequent reflective therapy sessions that reinforce these techniques.

If the client doesn´t receive a solid therapeutic explanation to their taxing experiences of anxiety there is a risk that anticipatory anxiety may be associated to an ever-increasing number of situations leading to generalized anxiety disorder (GAD). An unfortunate misconception, but probably pretty logical conclusion, that one of my patients stated when they were diagnosed with GAD was that "now, I´ll always have to live with anxiety".

The FRAMES model is client-focused and therefore easy to explain and apply in creative sessions, allowing insight into how psychological ill-health can develop but more importantly how we can act to maintain psychological well-being.

In summary: Therapy for anxiety should include teaching relevant physiological processes and allow for ample psychological reflection.

Using a systemic psychological overview provides an easy conduit for reflection on open existential questions but also allows for open association around human relations.

Nowadays, I usually discuss with my clients whether or not we should begin our sessions by going through relevant information about the autonomic nervous system and its constituent sympathetic and parasympathetic reflexes.

We discuss the role of breathing during panic attacks and compare it to respiratory function during strenuous physical activity.

In light of what my client brings up at the beginning of our interaction, various other functions in the FRAME overview may need to be brought to light at the start of therapy.

As therapy progresses, I encourage more open and diverse associations to my clients existential quandaries.

Stress reflexes i.e. sympathetic reflexes, are fundamental as a feed-back mechanism for the rest of our psyche.

Upon activation, fight or flight reflexes or if we freeze, our senses are alerted and focus on possible threats.

The sensory perceptions we zone in on are influenced by previous experiences, thoughts and actions that are associated with either traumatizing or pleasing events.

Brooding on experiences may eventually lead to worry and confusion.

Being able to reflect on worrisome thoughts with someone you trust can broaden your understanding about them and bring a sense of calm not only psychologically but also somatically.

Memories of critical incidents we have experienced can dominate our self-conception if we are left alone to process them.

Incomplete or simplified memories, associated with stress reactions can be reminiscent of an anxiety-generating event earlier in life.

Traumatizing memories that have been engrained through perception into our long-term memory may have a lasting effect on our lives.

This may in turn lead to our being caught up in mind-traps that affect us long-term. Angst-driven thoughts and feelings may be experienced as violations of our personal integrity.

I have occasionally encountered a reluctance on the part of clients and work-colleagues to acknowledge the important role the body plays in regulating inner stress, anxiety, phobia or compulsive urges whether it be in reaction to sudden psychological trauma or continual psycho-logical stress over long time.

In youth we tend to love the excitement of life.

That same lure of excitement might explain why it can take so long before we realize that we are on our way to being "burnt out" (exhaustion syndrome).

Generally speaking, from a societal point of view, it is important to decrease stress in the lives of those who have a hectic daily life, such as young parents and school personnel.

Business in contemporary society is primed to prioritize effectivity and competition. This provides a background stressor that can negatively affect a smooth family-life.

I would love to think that all parents were given ample time to spend, in a mindful way, with their offspring.

Advances in understanding the importance of sleep, recuperation, physical activity and having a well-balanced diet allow us all to gain a deeper understanding and respect for the importance of an optimal regulation of bodily needs to reach inner harmony.

The summary given in the next illustration shows that there are many factors that affect our well-being.

Physical trauma is not in the scope of this book. However, it is important to understand the stressful effect physical injury has on us, not only to deal with the effects of the injury itself but even its psychosocial consequences.

The interaction between our psyche and the given circumstances we have in life affect our ability to be joyful which is the opposite to being depressed.

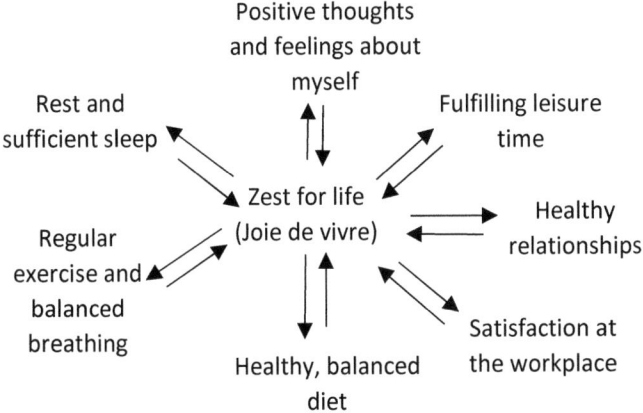

The seven parameters in the illustration optimize the ability to experience a zest for life which in turn makes it easier to exercise, eat healthily (ref. Eat to beat disease), find inner peace, pursue hobbies, develop good relationships and get on well in work.

We all benefit from understanding the relationship between stress reflexes, attention-focus and mind-traps.

We often construct a mind-trap by asking ourselves some question, for which there is no definite answer.

The young man with compulsive behavior (at the start of this chapter) needs the acknowledgement that physical exercise is good for him as an outlet to counteract the effects of stress.

81

However, the compulsive behavior represents an exaggerated reaction to corporal variations between sympathetic and parasympathetic activity.

Anxiety due to social fears or misconceptions about one´s body, may indeed be assuaged by perpetrating rituals and/or engaging in physical activity.

The calm experienced by engaging in compulsive acts is reward enough to reinforce such behavior.

However, if worrisome thoughts re-surface, the vicious cycle being relayed back and forth between compulsive thoughts and compulsive actions, is strengthened.

Compulsive thoughts can themselves lead to a vicious cycle through the mechanism of a negative feed-back loop between reflection and stress reflexes.

Although compulsive actions may decrease stress levels calming body and soul, in the long run, they may lead to a vicious cycle because a similar feed-back loop can also develop for other behaviors for example, alcohol dependency i.e. a ritualistic behavior is born.

You can compare it to the increasingly erratic and over-compensating casts a helicopter is subjected to when the pilot starts to lose control and over-compensates with his steering stick.

Anxiety, phobias and compulsive syndromes are fueled by thoughts that make the body uneasy.

When the level of fluctuations in worry due to compulsive thoughts and rituals reach a certain magnitude, the criteria for diagnosing compulsive syndrome are finally met, for example when a person's compulsive ritualistic behavior exceeds an hour a day.

Physical exercise and inner calm work well to diminish feelings of stress. Pumping out stress hormones during high-intensive physical exertion, such as bicycle-sprinting or other work-outs, leads to a state of relaxation and calm afterwards.

Mindfulness wherein attention is focused on what our sensory apparatus relays about our current external and internal state of affairs, allows our sensory impressions to come to the fore in gauging our "experience of self".

When our extracorporeal senses are allowed to relay the actual state of things it usually becomes apparent that everything is alright, despite our not feeling so on the inside.

Irrespective how physically active or still we are, being mindful supersedes rumination thereby lessening the risk for mind-traps. Worrying thoughts are pushed aside by pure cognizance and acceptance of the intracorporeal sensory impressions in the body.

Predominantly, no direct physical threats are present at this present point in time.

If brooding and pensive thought are allowed to dominate then there's a risk that we get caught in some default thoughts that cause apprehension and worry.

Taxing emotional cascades and worry due to post-traumatic stress inducing, catastrophic events, can be difficult to work through if we are not able to address them on the spot and begin processing the corporal stress reactions they spawned.

We might later try to re-instantiate those sensory experiences that we felt during a chocking event, in another context, as we try to process the chaotic event that befell us.

It's not necessarily so that we can remember all the sensory impressions associated with a shocking event, partly due to the selective nature of our attention.

As much as we can remember of the sensory impressions the likelihood that the same catastrophe may happen again is difficult to assess.

The uncertainty of the F-factor increases the risk for post-traumatic stress syndrome as the dynamics within the FRAMES model can be a hotchpotch of different questions that there are no definite answers to.

Mental reflections can be centered on another place and time but the sensory impressions and bodily reactions are happening at the present moment.

Many questions subsequent to traumatic experiences can be hard to answer if the F-factor is vague/diffuse.

Impact analysis

Behaviorisms greatest contribution to the science of psychology was its use of controlled scientific experiments around the relationship between cause and effect.

The development of behavioral therapy to cognitive behavioral therapy saw a shift from no longer solely focusing on behavioral change but even affording thoughts and feelings a deserved role in the therapy process.

My education in psychology in Umeå lay the emphasis on cognitive psychology and the psychology of learning, theory and research about learning concepts and skills.

In the infancy of behavioral therapy, the attitude of therapists was that everything would be fine if the client just trusted them and did what they told them to.

Feelings and thoughts were, for all intents and purposes, seen as irrational variables impossible to measure.

I found it hard to accept the prevailing culture of blindly accepting the tenets of this first wave of behavioral therapy.

What happens if the client doesn't trust the therapist or their experiences, thoughts and feelings thwart progress? Teachers in the gestalt therapy section, probably had the same experiences of behavioral therapy as I did.

During my education in gestalt therapy, teachers would stop me whenever it looked like I wanted to push a project with a client which was not based on that clients' own process. Just as well because the clients free will, feelings and consequentialist thinking are all central factors in their therapy process.

As a therapist, I must explain the associations I have that I feel have significance for the therapy process and let the client choose if they want to pursue that line of thought.

As with us all, the client's attention and perceptions are selective.

We notice certain people. We see various traits in their behavioral repertoire. Selectively, we either like or dislike what we observe. We show selectively what we think. The dynamics of FRAMES is all about selectivity and systemic consequences.

A child's selectivity can be expressed in its choice of toy in the playground. A grown-ups selectivity may be expressed in its affinity for a certain political party.

The fact that toddlers are more concrete in their thinking than adults shows that selectivity is differently formed in various phases of life.

Anil Seth's description of the psychosomatic interaction between outward-bound and inward-bound nerve signals illustrates the dynamic reciprocity within the psychological system.

Selectivity is fundamental to our psychodynamic process.

The selective process in our psyche becomes a comprehensive factor in how our future is formed. It is interwoven in our life tapestry. It encompasses past selectivity, future selective thinking and current selective thought.

The way we act and react leads to consequences.

Greek philosopher Socrates' central philosophical tenet was to "know yourself".

Adults tend to easily recognize the superficial consequences not only of teenagers but also of grown-ups behavior i.e. we think of the social consequences, what others will think of us.

Dynamic consequences within the whole FRAMES system are just as important for our psychological development and peace of mind.

In what way do our actions develop self-consciousness, empathy, morality, self-confidence and communicative skills?

What are the ramifications for us when we selectively only recognize the wishes of others as making us comfortable?

What are the consequences of not taking care of our physical health? What are the complications of too little sleep or physical exercise?

What is the impact of environmental pollution and global warming?

How consistent is our thinking in reality? Is there integrity in our actions? Do we allow automatized feelings to rule what we do?

Adults in therapy, who wish to develop themselves, will likely benefit the most by trying to adapt their behavior in a new way in the context they want to change.

Guilt can propagate change and development when it is associated with specific actions that are understood to be wrong whereas shame is vaguer and doesn't provide the same impetus for change.

Although teenagers consequential thinking gradually develops during their time at home, it is really only when they move away from home that they can and must take responsibility for making reflections on themselves and others.

Self-consciousness and insight into one´s own psyche increase with every snipping of the psychological umbilical cord to one´s parents /carers.

The prerequisites for consequential thinking and morality are built-in to our genetic make-up and neurophysiology as a result of our senses, the brains capacity for mental reflection, mirror neurons and the autonomic nervous system. Even small children are instinctively wired to react to injustices or nastiness.

On a purely biological plane, the brain continues to develop into adulthood. The brain has the ability to restructure and adapt by growing and learning, through experience, physiological maturation or degeneration. New experiences affect the brain throughout life.

Honesty and openness are positive conditions for promoting effective communication in all ages and relationships.

Fostering integrity and uniqueness in our relationships with others necessitates communication that respects both our own and other people's wishes.

In many circumstances it is considered important to be polite and courteous to our elders or those who of a more elevated social status.

By blindly following the will of others we risk losing ourselves.

Standards, ideals and morality have developed through the ages as a result of social interaction which formed a common concept of cause and effect and lay down a standard for what was considered to be good morals.

The formation of relationships throughout history have given us a common ground in understanding the mechanisms of cause and effect and have led to peoples adoption of an accepted sense of good morals.

Through thousands of years of social and collective interaction, in parties, ritual song, dance and trance, man has formed a notion of inner figures that we have imagined as gods.

The depiction of the gods of mankind being either good or bad is merely a projection of the corporal reactions of fight or flight reflexes, petrification, calm or being at peace.

The gods of war, love, creation, fertility etc. represent the different facets of the human condition.

The human psyches' use of inward- and outward-bound connections between the sensory apparatus and mental reflection logically leads us to project our thoughts to the outside world.

Our longing for an existential anchor outside ourselves has led to a collective demand for idols, gods and icons.

As an adult, I have understood that the Christian God I learned about in Sunday school was a manifestation of what the grown-ups wanted me to believe. However, I was not content to accept the type of God that was depicted in the Old Testament.

The God of the Bible demanded that Abraham prove his blind, unwavering loyalty by sacrificing his own son on the alter.

I came to conclusion that it is we who have created the gods in our minds, not the gods who have created us. This insight, my own morality and the reasoning and actions of those I have looked up to, have been the building blocks for my own personal belief system.

How can dreams that can be so illogical in content lead us to important insights?

I believe that it is because we don't censor ourselves when we dream.

In authoritarian contexts certain thoughts are taboo. Voicing particular thoughts may lead to negative consequences, socially.

Thoughts are one way when we are relaxed for example at night time or when we take a walk in the woods. They are of another kind in social situations where we have to be vigilant, especially in intolerant, strict environments.

Although, dreams may lack logical consistency logistically, i.e. they may not have realistic relevance in the sequence of events, they can still be relevant and encompass all the role-players in life.

A persons' feelings are real to that person whether they are experienced in dreams or in a woken state.

Being a responsible adult implies managing all of the facets of one´s own psyche: taking responsibility for making realistic and critical interpretations of what we observe, taking charge of our bodily well-being, our actions, our thoughts about our place in society and being responsible for how we express our feelings.

This accountability also entails being open for and aware of our own prejudices about ourselves and others.

We depend on each another in different ways, for survival the child is dependent on its parents, for emotional well-being we depend on our closest friends.

The fundamental method used in behavioral therapy is the examination of the relationship between context, actions and their consequences.

Insights into the detrimental consequences of conditioned dysfunctional behavior can motivate us to a new way of thinking and learning.

The main focus of object relation theory is to examine our experiences in close relationships.

In the 45 years I spent working as a psychologist in different organizations I have always thought that both of these fundamental theoretical veins of thought do not need to be mutually exclusive.

Can clients who find psychotherapy based on object-relations helpful, necessarily, not find behavioral therapy helpful, and vice versa?

Based on my experience, I'd say that we need to deepen our understanding of which modes of therapy our clients tend to choose and find helpful. The choice of therapy modality is strongly dependent on how satisfactory the rapport between the client and therapist is.

Theory is one thing, practice quite another. Building rapport and establishing a good working relationship between client and therapist are essential to successful therapeutic work.

Integrating the best elements of both psychological schools of thought can allow the psychotherapist to offer each patient the most suitable mode of treatment based on their particular stage of development.

The behavioral scientific tradition was based on controlled experiments with animals.

The school of thought promulgated by Freud was based on his hypothesizing about the cases he had, in an era where sexual education was taboo.

In effect, subsequent theoretical conflicts have led to a long-lasting polarization between well-structured CBT on one hand and open associations based the client/therapist dialogue, on the other hand.

Even if you have lived through chaotic and horrific object relationships, it is possible to develop psychologically through re-learning in a new way and by nurturing healthier relationships.

For context, look up Christina Lejonöga and Annica Ljungs book, "Leva nu: om trauma & dissociation" (2018).

My breakthrough in finding self-empathy (compassion/harmony) came during a course in gestalt therapy when I played both roles.

In one chair sat a slouching Staffan, who ever since childhood tackled periods of mild depression.

In the other chair sat self-critical Staffan.

After a while, I stood up and reviewed the dialogue from a third perspective. Introvertly, I saw that they matched each other perfectly.

They were dependent on each other. Without self-critical Staffan there would have been less self-critique and shame. Without depressed Staffan, Self-critical Staffan would not have had the right environment for offensive, degrading self-critique.

Body and soul are intertwined. The state of our bodily health has an impact on our psyche as does the perception we have of our bodies impact the functioning of our lives, spiritually.

An obvious example of this is how we are more content when we are full-up than when we are hungry. Another example is how we feel happier after a walk than after a day full of stress at work.

We feel better after a good night's sleep than after having slept badly.

When I have focused on physiological events in the body, especially on the effect breathing has on anxiety, I have sometimes noted clients surprise and reluctance to focus on physiological phenomena instead of psychological aspects. This may be due to the perception that balanced breathing, sleep, diet and exercise are the focus of medical doctors, not psychologists.

People expect to talk about relationship problems with their psychotherapist.

In my striving to encourage client input in sessions, I ask if it´s ok if I sketch a framework to address their anxiety, insomnia and stress which for many clients lead to burn-out or depression.

The body can't bear the burden of being in a constant state of stress if the burden isn't counteracted with sufficient peace and quiet i.e. enough recuperation and quality sleep.

What happens to relationships in which people are not physically healthy? What happens to the body when relationships are unwell?

Our physiological make-up is a system of different, mutually interdependent parameters. Our psychological profile also consists of parameters that are interwoven with each other.

The psyche and body are systemically interdependent and reflect different perspectives of us.

When I started working at the youth health clinic, I was very fortunate to work in a tight knit team who were familiar with, supported and respected each other's professional boundaries.

This gave me a unique opportunity to create a pedagogical framework for treatment of anxiety that was based on psychological and corporal science.

The open and creative atmosphere that was generated in this, Sweden's first ever Youth health clinic, made this possible.

FRAMES-analysis

When I started drawing up a FRAME-overview on the white-board, different factors ended up in different places on the chart depending on how the discourse developed.

Originally, I simply wanted a functional communication between myself and my client. Some clients preferred to communicate verbally, others liked having the visual support of the white-board. Sometimes I wrote and drew, other times my client did.

Open association and petrifying anxiety are polar opposites. If creative dialogue is allowed to dominate, we can allow free and open thought to flourish, encouraging more open dialogue.

I begin the FRAMES-analysis by highlighting the main focus points that are developed from my open questions.

Subsequently, I ask more specific questions.

What did you notice in that situation? What did you think? How did you feel? What did you do? What happened after that?

Writing down points of reference make it easier to analyze cause and effect as the main points of the clients' stories, including their systemic consequences, become apparent.

Just as perceptions affect our thoughts, so too, do our thoughts affect our focus of attention.

Just as perceptions can agitate us, can a feeling of agitation affect what we pay attention to.

Similar to how stress affects our actions can our actions cause us stress.

In the same way our actions can affect our thoughts, our thoughts can affect how we behave.

Emotions affect what we think about, as do our thoughts affect how we feel, and so on.

All of these reciprocal connections form a psycho-somatic dynamic whole that represents the dynamics found in our most important body part, the brain.

Shedding light on certain systemic connections can be threatening. Therefore, the development pace of the therapeutic process is an important parameter. "You can't wade out into a river and make it flow faster or slower".

When sensory perceptions become apparent, for example in gestalt therapeutic role-play or when you draw and speak, it's easy to be present in that moment.

Feelings of anxiety are less paralyzing during therapy, provided we can act in some way towards them.

The most obvious sign of depression is when you don't want to do anything at all, not even things that you used to find so enjoyable.

Anxiety and depression are intervariable. I have noticed, while analyzing results from the "Hospital Anxiety and Depression Scale" that those youths who scored higher on the depression scale than the anxiety scale, had, in general, suffered from anxiety for a long time.

The exhaustion of constantly feeling anxiety, over a long period of time, without sufficient rest and recuperation became very evident when clients completed the self-assessment form, "Karolinska Exhaustion Disorder Scale".

What should we do if we lose the will to live life?

Considering that the psyche is a system of mutually interconnected functions, it is important to try to understand how all the various factors affect each other interdependently, in the dynamic FRAMES-system.

Using the psychosocial overview on page 81, we can see that the will to live varies depending on what conditions you're living in, as a whole.

There's a lot of evidence that regular exercise leads to the quickest and most durable effect on anxiety and depression (look up the book "Hjärnstark" in the list of references).

In my contact with youths at the health clinic I learned that the worrying thoughts that some experienced were associated with corporal memories.

We perceive many more sensory impressions than those from our environment. Through interoception we also receive a multitude of sensory reactions within the body.

What do we mean by "sixth sense"? Possibly, it's the so-called "gut-feeling".

Pain experienced in the neck, stomach, shoulders or back can all have different etiologies; poor sitting posture, psychological stress and so on.

Body posture and breathing pattern can be associated with sensations and memories stored physically in the body. These can cause pain in different parts of the body depending on what memories are elicited from external or internal sensory perceptions.

To examine the relationship between body sensations and external or internal stress factors, I engaged with some of my young clients in the following exercise which was partly inspired by a workshop with Gay and Kathlyn Hendricks who have written the book At the Speed of Life.

Before the exercise I asked for their permission to do an exercise and described how it was carried out.

I used a figure that had a thought bubble that I nearly always drew on the whiteboard, to illustrate how sensory perceptions and thoughts can make us uneasy or calm.

An upward pointing arrow represented agitation, a downward pointing arrow symbolized relaxation.

Then I wrote down some thought or information in the thought bubble that riled my client up, in fear, aggression, infatuation or some other experience that caused a spike in autonomic, sympathetic activity in the body.

I also drew reciprocal arrows between the thoughts in the bubbles and corporal reactions in the body.

Each thought bubble could only contain a single stressing factor. Other stressors would be put on a list for later analysis).

After that my client reclined his seat and settled himself comfortably. He put one hand on his ribcage and one on his tummy, just above the belly button.

Then I asked him; "which hand moves when you breathe?"

If the hand on the belly was the one that moved I confirmed that that was the way it should be when we breathe calmly and are relaxed.

If it was mainly the hand on the ribcage that moved I said: "If you want to feel more relaxed, improving your breathing pattern can help you."

Often it was the clients who specifically sought help for panic-attacks who showed very apparent ribcage breathing.

After that we went through a progressive relaxation technique with successive focus on the body's muscles.

If it was the first time we performed the relaxation exercise, I helped the client to focus by firstly tensing and then relaxing different muscle groups in sequence; the muscles of the feet, legs, buttocks, back, neck, forehead, jaws and around the eyes.

When my client had achieved a state of relaxation throughout the body and was breathing calmly, they judged their stress level on a 10 point calm/stress scale. Then I asked my client to think about one of the stressors I had written down on the whiteboard.

During the exercise, after having reminded the client of one of their stressors, my client was asked to describe in what part of the body they experienced the most agitation. Subsequently, I asked the client to focus on that part of the body.

After that I asked my client to raise the level of that feeling in their body and then to lower it.

Their level of success varied. Examining corporal memories requires concentration and time.

By focusing and being patient, some clients managed to gain the ability to increase and/or decrease some particular sensation in their bodies.

The nature of our sensory apparatus in relaying and reinforcing stimuli leads to our noticing and prioritizing that which stresses us the most.

When a thought arouses us, certain corporal sensations can be amplified.

While I was receiving radiation treatment for prostate cancer, I noticed that my experience of pain varied a lot depending on what I was doing, thinking about or was concentrating on.

If I put something unpleasant out of my mind, I don't get concerned/agitated in the same way as when I'm consumed by some worrying thought.

Corporal experiences can be heightened by mental reflections and reciprocally, mental reflections can in turn amplify corporal experiences. This is due to the interdependent nature of communication between the brain and the body, where information travels in both directions, back and forth.

This is the case with my tinnitus, for example. I can generally put it out of my mind when I'm not specifically concentrating on it.

Body sensations provide input to the brain. A sensation that is dwelled upon can become a misdirected thought.

A client at the clinic who was well-investigated medically, for heart palpitations was referred to me due to his anxiety and apprehension about experiencing episodes. He found it hard to believe that it was his own apprehension for having palpitations that itself generated actual, stress-induced palpitations.

One week when he had the flu and high fever, he felt better than he had done for ages. We surmised that he was so tired and exhausted that he didn't have the time nor the energy to even think about palpitations, let alone worry about them.

Inner stress, sensory impressions, cognition and emotion, all help form experiences as a whole. That is reflected in the way we do what we want to do, and we don't do what we do not want to do.

Having a holistic experience of oneself might explain the positive effect of placebo in those who have only taken placebo pills without an active ingredient.

Positive expectations affect the FRAMES dynamics (a holistic blueprint of ourselves). It affects our perception of internal and external sensory impressions, the autonomic nervous system, our actions, thoughts and feelings.

When I am tuned in and aware of the situation, the sum of sensory perceptions and mental associations I make, allow me to be calm and harmonic.

In addition, if I am engaged in some sensomotory activity, in line with my current energy level, it is even easier to feel healthy and well. Activities such as cycling, walking in the woods or even eating a sandwich in the great outdoors, can all be experienced as things that increase the quality of life.

Interoception, perception, physiological reactions, mental reflections, emotions and actions all are part of and interact in a dynamic psychosomatic oneness.

The aim of this exercise was to help my client understand that thoughts and feelings are separate entities that can be focused on individually and they can also be the generator of one other.

Todays' problems with confirmation bias and fact resistance can probably be explained by the inner picture we have of ourselves and the confirmation of that picture through reinforcement in social media networks and social relationships we are integrated in.

It's possible to understand the reluctance to change the dynamics of our own personal FRAMES, if we embrace that what we feel inside (through the dynamics of group and societal interaction) are interacting complex systems that are difficult to clearly comprehend.

If we belong to a tight knit group in school, at work or in a hobby group, a certain pressure to adhere to the beliefs and attitudes prevalent in that group, make it hard to act differently than the norms accepted within that "pack".

Body language, mimicry, verbal interaction and behavior mediated via the senses through mirroring neuronal activity, can lead to individuals in a group mirroring each other's reactions when changes occur that affect the groups' subjective reality.

Accordingly, the dynamics present in one persons' psyche may be transmitted to other persons in a group or family (please refer to the overview on the next page).

The group-dynamic is an enigmatic phenomenon. Although group dynamics can be defined in terms of the teachings of group psychology (the common goals of and atmosphere in the group, the camaraderie, the values held by the group and so on) it is important to highlight the specific psychodynamic processes operating within all the group members, individually.

Individual psychodynamics forge a group dynamic that can be explained using the connection link FRAMES (see next page).

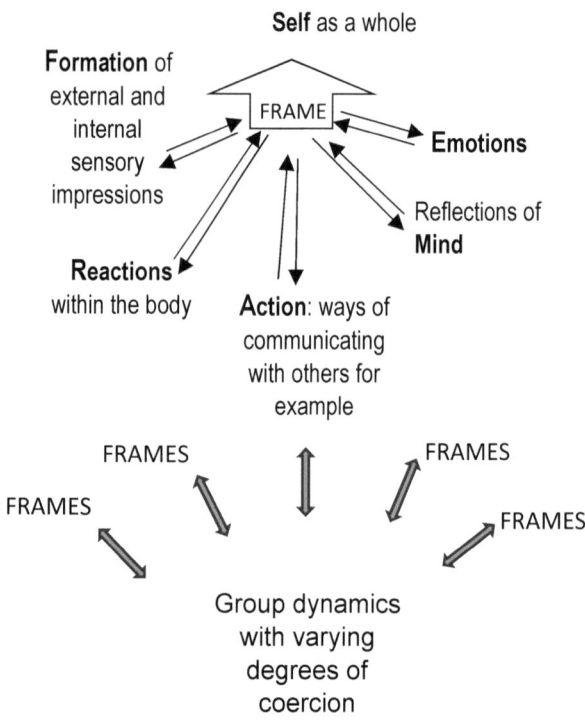

The group dynamic is formed by the random interaction of all the group members' own particular psychodynamic processes.

The systemic effect is reciprocal, with the individual affecting the group and the group, in turn, affecting the individual.

The journey to becoming an independent person with self-esteem, who can maintain boundaries is variable in the different group environments of the family or wider, social and cultural structures.

Managing our own psychodynamic dissonance requires an awareness of the dissonance prevalent in the specific groups to which we belong and to the dissonance existing on a societal level, as a whole.

For example, the addict who strives to break free from the drugs environment he lives in but finds it too hard, is a vivid illustration of the difficulty in placing boundaries between oneself and the group to which one belongs.

If a client with a phobia for taking lifts tries to tackle the phobia by getting in the lift but then says "it's too hard", I usually ask if it's a thought or a feeling they are experiencing.

When my client has taken a moment to think about it, the answer is usually that it's both.

Obviously that is the case but it's a good idea to reflect on the possible reasons why someone might or might not, be ready to act for a change in behavior. Corporal memories? Mind-traps? Traumatic memories? Inner identity? Projected identity? Self-criticism? Loyalty to the group? Inner stress? Stressed breathing pattern?

An experience can imprison your mind, hold you in a vice grip of FRAME-factors that are inexorably intertwined, locking you in a FRAMES-trap.

Allowing things to remain locked and function automatically, make it difficult to accept and believe in the need for change, even if you have felt bad for a long time.

By analyzing a FRAMES-trap and coming up with possible strategies to extract yourself from it, the possibility for you break free from the trap presents itself.

The best way to break free from a FRAMES-trap is to experiment with new ways of acting and behaving. This increases the likelihood of succeeding because new ways of behaving tend to generate new sensory impressions, different interpretations, alternate body sensations, mental reflections and emotions.

We can break habitual reasoning patterns by prioritizing and imposing *our own will* first. Then we can focus our attention accordingly.

It was quite a challenge to persuade my young clients to immerse themselves in the experiences they had, using a wider perspective that took into account corporal, social and psychological factors.

If they succeeded, it would give them a sense of coherence with which they could take charge of the situation.

The description of psychological context that I outline in this book is more abstract and theoretical compared to the more practical, concrete work I did with the youths that sought my help.

I wanted to help my clients as much as I could to understand their experiences in a wider perspective and approach them using their own notions and vocabulary.

The way we perceive external and internal sensory impressions is an important factor in our psychological development. Another important factor is our reaction to stress.

Action is a third. Mental reflection is a fourth factor. Feelings/emotions a fifth factor in peoples' psychology.

Our perception of the interaction of these diverse functions forms an inner picture in our minds of how we act.

Youths generally experience a lot of extrinsic and intrinsic stress factors.

Physiologically, changes in hormone activity in their bodies are greatly amplified compared to previous childhood years. Some teenagers grow so fast that they suffer growing pains and have problems with co-ordination.

Synchronization between the motor structures in the brain and the executive functioning of the extremities is hampered due to the increased speed in body growth.

Due to powerful changes in hormonal activity, it´s common to hear teenage boys' voices breaking and to see how young teenage girls develop more feminine body features.

Trauma from early childhood can be rekindled in the teenage years but this period of change can also provide great opportunities to form new, more healthy, subject relations.

Teenagers may temporarily regress to some earlier childhood phase and then suddenly behave as though they were grown-ups again.

A beloved teddy-bear from childhood or a certain song you love to listen to can function to provide you some comfort. Just behaving childishly with friends can also be a release.

In school, group affiliation can shift from year to year. Children are subjected to extrinsic stress factors at home and in school.

The natural inquisitiveness, creativity and open-mindedness that youths generally possess, provide an important function in transitioning to adult life.

The self-analysis we adults engage in, helps us discover possible FRAMES blockages, which allows us to work though anxiety and/or depression, thus providing the impetus for developmental change.

Adaptation of mental reflections

The scientific theorist, Jean Piaget, outlined how cognitive development occurs in leaps due to the interaction between assimilation (incorporation of sensory input with current cognition) and accommodation (adaptation of cognition).

Realizing the presence of cognitive dissonance and handling it maturely, is an integral component in fostering advances in personal development.

Integrating Piaget's conclusions in my FRAMES model, I deduced the following:

In FRAMES psychodynamics, the six separate psychological FRAMES functions are all influenced by and adapted to each other. In effect, this means that we are inclined to hone our attention in such a way that our habitual way of seeing things is confirmed (confirmation bias).

An anxiety mind-trap that perpetuates our thinking in the same anxiety fueling manner, may block spontaneous creativity.

Therefore, when the psyche is obviously being dissonant, we need to take a leap in our psychological development, we need to adjust our FRAMES dynamics.

I sometimes offer the following as an example of accommodation: when we notice that the same amount of water seen in a tall, thin glass, strangely appears to be different when it's poured into a lower, wider glass, we are forced to adjust our thought process.

Initially, we try to explain what we actually see but can't. The apparent contradiction of how the water from one of the glasses actually looks less in the glass that appears to be smaller, forces us to make a cognitive leap of growth in order to solve the mysterious experience. However, the optical "illusion" can subsequently be explained by employing substantiating sensomotory and auditory reflection, instantiating the sudden ex-perience of "a eureka moment".

If someone we respect and trust confirms that we have, finally understood the concept of volume, we experience positive feed-back that affirms us. The eureka moment amplifies our curiosity and thereby encourages further developmental leaps.

Development of cognition (ability to abstract thinking) probably affects perspectival self, narrative self, volitional self and social self, but how?

The matrix below generates a number of hypotheses for basic psychological research. How do developments in mental reflection impact FRAMES factors?

	Childhood	Youth	Adulthood
F	1	2	3
R	4	5	6
A	7	8	9
M	10	11	12
E	13	14	15
S	16	17	18

The last letter (S) on the y axis of the table above represents the entire experience we have of ourselves (self-esteem, self-confidence, self-respect and self-image).

The example I gave of the glasses of water describing the concept of volume is represented in box one in the table (formation of optical impressions) and box ten (mental reflection).

Everyone experiences crises as they develop, for example during puberty or when we move out on our own. These events in the transition from childhood to adulthood, affect all FRAMES functions.

Breakthroughs in comprehension and skills can occur in early childhood, teenage years and adulthood. We gain knowledge about our bodies, feelings, perceptual, cognitive and motor skills.

Every individual has to face a unique set of challenges that arise over the years. The challenges are caused by the individuals' earlier experiences and the diverse circumstances that each individual faces.

An emotional crisis, such as the break-up of a relationship, also affects all the FRAMES functions.

The consequences of such a crisis, fundamentally alters the way we perceive our body, our feelings, our environment, our volition, our self-image, our behavior and how others see us.

Due to various circumstances including impaired physical function or psychosocial handicaps children at the habilitation center made developmental leaps at different stages in their maturing process. For example, some children had remarkably uneven result profiles. They could have very high scores in the Whechsler Intelligence Test for children and yet have low scores in some of the other tests.

Accepting your lot is a prerequisite to being mindful and in harmony with yourself and your environment.

Spiritual harmony is dependent on diverse factors in our lives: the relationships we have with others, conditions experienced during formative years, emotional and/or physical form on a given day and our level of psychological maturity.

The FRAMES model provides a frame of reference for analyzing yourself, your memories and thoughts about the future as well as your current self-perception.

Present day experiences can generate associations to events earlier in life or to thoughts about the future.

Mindfulness of oneself, here and now, is easier to achieve if we remain calm in the presence of thoughts associated with events that occurred earlier in life or events that we are anxious might happen in the future.

Acceptance of these thoughts makes it easier to revert our attention to the present and what we are experiencing now, allowing us to disregard things that have happened in the past or that could happen in the future.

Thoughts about other events and places can trigger stress reflexes that are associated with embarrassing or painful memories. Thoughts about the future can give rise to apprehension and anxiety but even to feelings of enthusiasm and elation (autonomic sympathetic reactions).

It has become apparent to me that if I use of all of my FRAME constituents, it facilitates self-regulation of my thought process and how I feel as a whole.

Probably my most important insight is how the interaction between extrinsic and intrinsic sensory stimuli works and the fact that self-esteem varies depending on the context in which I find myself.

The diverse and complex nature of our psychology is seen in popular YouTube videos where toddlers start crying the first time they see their formerly bearded fathers, clean shaven. Their dismay is a form of shock caused by the fact that they have only ever seen their father with a beard.

The child has yet to develop object constancy in respect to its father.

The child cannot reconcile the mental picture it has of its father with how its father looks without a beard.

The child's perception at this particular point in time doesn't match its expectations. It experiences FRAMES dissonance, a great difference between its expectations and reality and starts to cry.

When the child is calmer, it can examine its daddy's new appearance.

Adults can experience dissonance when listening to politicians who have totally different opinions about society than they themselves have.

The FRAMES dissonance in adults is generated by the incompatibility between the feelings they are registering and their sensory impressions, whether or not they are extrinsic or intrinsic.

I like to compare FRAME dissonance to an out of tune five string instrument that has one string untuned. In other words, the FRAMES chord is out of tune.

Cognitive dissonance implies that contradictory thoughts give rise to discomfort and apprehension.

FRAMES dissonance implies inconsistency between any one of the FRAME strings.

The other day, when I was being mindful, I got a vague tingling feeling of worry despite being off work for the day. I wanted to try and describe that feeling in words.

The first word that came to mind was "rushed" despite the fact that there was nothing that had to be done urgently.

The R string quivered (stress heightened). The M string, the feeling that I am in a hurry to do something, shook even though I had nothing to do that required urgent attention. There was no specific goal I had to achieve without delay. The A string was strained to its limits but silent.

The chord sounded discordant.

When a friend told me that he also had that worried, tingling sensation of inner stress, I asked him what he called it.

He answered "drive".

Drive was another word to describe the same sensation and a word that I would adopt as it particularly suited my disposition. The intent of the word driven has a positive connotation that suits my personality better than the word rushed, which has a negative implication.

What should I do when I feel this sensation?

My imaginative friend compared my apprehension to being afflicted by a psychological "computer virus".

The analogy of a stringed instrument sounding out of tune can also be used to encapsulate the problem.

FRAMES-development, being an all-encompassing description of development of self, might be useful in analyzing the problem, arriving at a plausible explanation for it and suggesting a possible solution to it.

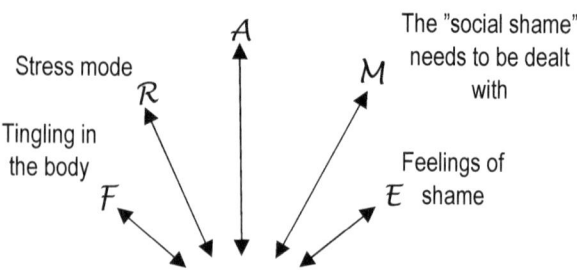

Eager readiness for action

A

Stress mode
R

The "social shame"
needs to be dealt
with
M

Tingling in
the body
F

Feelings of
E shame

I have a "social drive" in me, but now
above all I want to feel balance and
harmony within myself

When I read Marta Cullberg Weston's book "Från skam till självrespekt", I realized that I was occasionally subject to white shame, i.e., the sort of shame that's integrated in one´s self-esteem early on in life which lies latent like a psychological virus ready to cause problems.

In private, I've been told that it's as if I had a "switch" that turns on or off when I'm interacting with people.

When the white shame is activated due to some early memory, the flow of associations to it is turned off. I freeze. I can't be reached.

128

I can't explain why but the feeling of shame scrambles normal communication when the subject matter is emotionally sensitive.

I have now created an image in my mind of an alteration switch that I can control. It can represent a transformer of associations, an anti-virus programme, appropriately enough, as its concept came to me based on my friends' reflections.

This inner image of the alteration switch has facilitated a developmental leap in my psyche, allowing med to turn the flow of associations back on and drop the feeling of shame.

The E string has for the greater part of my life made my self-consciousness disharmonious.

The feeling of shame has dogged me for as long as I can remember and now that I'm aware of it I want to escape it.

It's no longer a fight to be fought as I choose to take a step back, reflect and accept myself for who I am. I accept what I am experiencing at this very point in time.

Dissonance can give us the motivation to be interested in our own psychology, to develop ourselves mentally and search for ways to find harmony in our lives.

Through self-analysis, I have realized that my internalized shame is derived from forbidden aggression. I must stop forbidding that feeling. When I accept the feeling, especially if it's un-warranted, it seems to lose its energy.

Doctrine taught in gestalt therapy classes inform us that we integrate polarities within ourselves. The problem with aggression is one where we are torn between rage and timidity.

In order to integrate my polarizing aggression, I need to practice the ability of moving effortlessly along the scale of aggression, allowing myself to adapt the level of my belligerence to suit the gravity of the situation at hand i.e., be a little angry, pretty angry and so on, concordant with the circumstances.

We all have good and bad sides within us. From birth we have pre-programmed reflexes: fight or flight, freezing (petrification), being capable of being calm and relaxed.

In social interaction, we need to regulate both sides of the autonomic nervous system. It is very im-portant that parents allow their children to feel the full gamut of emotions.

That doesn't mean that parents should allow their children to behave any way they please but they should accept the child's various feelings so that the child itself can accept those feelings. It is also important for parents to comfort and help their child to identify their feelings.

Sometimes, I actually need my aggression, for example when I have to find the energy to complete some physically challenging work.

The psychology of learning proposes that random amplification of actions/behavior in different situations makes it harder to understand if we are on the right track or not.

Consequential amplification facilitates our ability to handle the situations we face.

Object relations theory describes the important development towards so-called object permanence, i.e., the child's comprehension that mother exists despite not being able to see her. The child understands that mother is one and the same person despite the dichotomy of her sometimes being a source of frustration and ire while at other times, the one who evokes feelings of love and satisfaction.

The road to respectful, effective communication with others, requires us to take responsibility for our own psychodynamics and boundaries while also showing respect for the boundaries and wishes of others.

In all my years as a psychologist, I have noticed that it is difficult for me to instill in my clients the insight, that their selectively directed attention is a progenitor of the mind-traps they have, associated with fear and/or aggression.

I often interpreted my clients' problems as being chiefly derived from a complex array of mind-traps, heated emotions and dysfunctional behavior.

The problem of coerced consensus of opinion in groups such as school classes can be exacerbated by the effect of gossip on the group dynamic.

Children can understand this phenomenon by participating in the following exercise:

With the students sitting in a ring, the teacher whispers a sentence to one of them, who in turn whispers the same sentence to the next one. When the sentence has been passed on by all the students and comes back to the first child, it is usually altered in some way and in proportion to the length of the sentence.

The difference in meaning between the first and last sentence can be explained by each students own interpretation of the words and how they use their own words to express it.

By changing only one small detail in the sentence or by using another choice of words the original meaning is altered slightly.

That change may then grow as the message is forwarded. The gossip effect increases the discrepancy and, accordingly, the message becomes distorted as it is sent forth within the ring.

If a gossiped "truth" finds anchor and becomes a superficial truth within the group, it can cause major problems. In a group characterized by a sense of insecurity, tension is heightened as the members find it hard to establish the true feelings, opinions and intentions of the one gossiped about.

You and me

The core to relationships is the interaction between individuals who each have their own specific psychological and subjective reality.

The involved parties have their own experience of a relationship and how they feel that they are treated by the other. Each of them is the object of the others attention, emotions and thoughts while simultaneously being the active subject with their own selective perceptions, feelings and thoughts about the other.

The evolution of psychology as a science has been fueled by the need to understand ourselves and others. Self-awareness gives us the insight that others too, have self-awareness.

Every person develops their own theory of mind.

Friedrich "Fritz" Perls and Laura Posner-Perls who laid the foundations of Gestalt therapy, coined the so-called gestalt prayer that reflected their thoughts about individuality within relationships.

"I do my thing, you do yours. I'm not in this world to live up to your expectations. You're not in this world to live up to my expectations."

You are you. I am me. If we happen to connect, that's beautiful. If not, so be it.

I lack self-love when I forego myself in order to please you. I lack love for you when I try to make you be the way I want you to be, instead of accepting you as you are. You are you and I am me".

The poem describes the relationship between two adults. In different mutual, relationships such as familial relationships or those between employer and employee, the mutual interaction can be experienced as safe or insecure, just or unjust.

The security found in this interdependency comes from each individuals' self-perception. The following overview shows various types of dependency:

	Children´s dependence	Adult´s dependence
For survival	The young child´s dependence on adult care	Social and economic understandings
For emotional well-being	The child´s emotional attachment	The adult´s emotional attachment

Small children must be cared for in order to survive. They need support in their physical, mental and emotional development.

In families, social networks and indeed all aspects of societal life we need the interaction with others.

Logically, behavior is a central component in cognitive behavioral therapy.

I prefer the term action because action best describes the experience of yourself as an actor with the ability to influence the relationships you find yourself in.

Compare the sentences, "tomorrow I will behave another way" with "tomorrow I will act another way".

Similarly, I have found it hard to accept the term object which is fundamental to object relation theory as that word distracts attention from the fact that we are talking about real people, of flesh and blood, living and interacting with each other.

In my work at the youth health center, the concepts of behavioral science became the cornerstones of the FRAMES model I formed to give an explanatory outline of key functions of our psychology.

Instead of using the word stimulus in behavioral analysis, I thought that word like *notice* or pay attention to were more appropriate when talking about the experience of extrinsic and intrinsic stress factors in life. This made it easier to consider and talk of alternative interpretations of what the youths had perceived.

Sometimes, the youths wondered about their interpretations of things that important people in their lives had once said or done.

Perception and attention became an integral part of the psychological analysis of my young clients' family and school life.

In therapy, external, provocative elements could then be associated to their corporal reactions, actions, reflections and feelings.

Thus, it became easier for the youths to talk about their experiences of themselves instead of focusing on the behavior of their class-mates, parents or other people.

It is crucial to have of an understanding of our own psychological processes i.e. an awareness of our own role in relationships.

A lot has happened in the field of object relations theory since Freud instigated its development.

Also, the foundations of behavioral sciences put forth by Pavlov and Skinner have been extensively built on since they were popularized.

For a long time, I deliberated on how to build a theoretical bridge to span the gap between the frames of reference of behaviorists and those of object relations theorists.

Hopefully, a common framework to integrate both theories can be found by applying the variable of selectively directed attention, to the object relation theory's analysis of object relations and behavioral therapist's analysis of thought, feeling and action.

Integrating the Freudian and the behavioral science trains of thought must be characterized by a sense of good will.

Research on the amygdala and its fight, freeze or flight reflexes can contribute to behavioral and object relation therapists' understanding of anxiety.

In the analysis of relationships the concept of "you and I" can be transcribed to the words object and subject.

In order to facilitate an explanation of the dramatic contents of events, I occasionally use the word "main character" synonymously with "subject".

Inner object gestalts formed in previous relationships with persons we were once dependent on, can thwart the harmony of relationships we experience with people in the present.

Former gestalts can distort experiences of new acquaintances we currently relate to.

The subject's perception of a new object can be clouded if its attention and thoughts are prejudiced by former inner objects.

If the subject hopes or fears that a new object will confirm its own opinions or prejudices about itself, there is an increased probability of egocentric selectivity in its interaction with the new object.

Inner object gestalts, whether old or new, can be incrementally distorted as time goes by.

This may happen irrespective of whether communication is poorly performed or terminated altogether, due to the egocentric perceptual bias of one or both of the people in a relationship.

In order to address this, the individuals involved must try to find an overall perspective of the relationship, advisedly with the help of a third party.

While analyzing a mutual relationship, it's important to consider the interaction from both the perspective of the subject and the object.

Role-play in gestalt therapy, with two empty chairs as props, allows the participant to physically change perspective in a relationship, even when the other party is not present.

In one chair you can express one of the subjective perspectives, in the other chair the others' imagined subjective perspective. Accordingly, you can switch between chairs, thus developing inner dialogue.

In object relations theory, *projective identification* is the term used for projection and hiding from one's own feelings.

Projective identification is an important and enlightening psychological mechanism that we are each aware of, in varying degrees.

Using body-language, mimicry and different tones of voice we project our own perceptions, needs and feelings onto those we interact with believing them to then have the same perceptions, needs and feelings. Projection involves a myriad of different feelings from positive to negative.

Among other things, projective identification can be used to explain the mechanism of curling. The parent projects a need for help onto the child even though the child hasn't asked for or even needs help. The child's retort that they can do it themselves should be respected, as it is their wish to act independently and show their own ability.

The parent has to perform a balancing act by helping the child in such a way that it instills in it a sense of security and self-esteem, while at the same time not thwarting its development and self-competence.

Projective identification as a relational phenomenon within psychology can also be instrumental in causing passive or active bullying.

A large number of patients that I've treated, in my role as a therapist throughout the years, have had the experience of being bullied.

Years later, when they finally had gained perspective to their experience of being bullied, they were ready to tackle and work through the negative feelings, caused by being outcast and ridiculed. They could see the detrimental effect it had had on their self-esteem.

In my work as a school psychologist, I found that bullies were often willing to talk to those who felt bullied, but the bullied individual in turn, were not open to talking to the bullies.

If bullying is seen as the transfer and counter transmission of reluctance, it becomes even more apparent how complicated feelings of ostracization are, as a phenomenon within group dynamics.

Individual A, experiences reluctance to individual B, by projecting the feeling of reluctance on individual B.

Although A can certainly identify the feeling of reluctance, he/she is unaware of his/her own feeling of reluctance towards B.

Reciprocally, B readily feels reluctance towards A, in a retaliatory feeling of reluctance.

The complex dynamics of benevolence and mal-evolence need to be highlighted, analyzed and understood in terms of the object relations theoretical concepts of projection and counter-projection of feelings through tone of voice, mimicry and body language. This allows us to better understand the relational problems experienced in couples, groups and society at large.

The British psychiatrist and psychoanalyst, John Bowlby, explored a new psychological field of research in the 1950 s', that later developed the concept of attachments, early and later in life.

Research by the American developmental psychologist, Mary Ainsworth established the psychological concepts of secure attachment, insecure avoidance attachment and insecure ambivalent attachment.

I believe that during projective identification in child birth, the emotional processes in the mother are communicated in a deluge of emotion through the mutual contact with the newborn baby. This identification and projection of love is a special bond formed between mother and child.

The newborns primary relation to its mother consists of its actions, its mother's reactions and the subsequent interaction between them both. Recurring questions in the mother's consciousness of herself surface and the child's development towards independence is instigated.

The newborns sensory motor and emotional activity along with its relationship to its mother, starts to form directly after birth.

What does the mother notice? How does she react? What actions does she take? What thoughts and emotions are going through her mind?

Should the child for some reason shun the food offered, it can affect the mother's sense of security in her attachment to the child and vice versa. This can be detrimental to the initial, sensitive attachment phase in the child's life.

There may be multiple reasons for the child's unwillingness to suckle, for example it may have a gag reflex or maybe it's allergic to breast milk or formula, or perhaps the feeding environment is not calm and secure. In order to help the child, the mother can take responsibility for the situation by trying to understand the child's difficulties.

She uses all her extrinsic and intrinsic senses to observe the child.

She can perceive the child as an inner object in two respects: one is her general perception of how to take care of children, the other is what she imagines it would be like to actually be the child that she is currently nursing in her arms.

If the mother interprets her own body signals negatively or if she has too much focus on the child's experience of nursing and is unaware of her own self-perception, it can have ramifications for their mutual experience of attachment.

Initially, the child's experience of its own body and its mother's is indistinguishable. The child is enveloped by its mother's state of health and actions as well as the other physical conditions it is a part of.

What does mother think and feel as she nurses her little baby? Can she deal with possible stress reactions in the child and within herself? Can she console the baby and herself?

I expect that mutual contact and social interaction between children and their fathers can similarly be claimed to involve projective identification.

Subsequently, memories are formed of the interaction between the child and the rest of its family.

The relationship between parents and their child results in the parents' extrinsic and intrinsic sensory perceptions being relayed to the child's sensory perceptions, thereby forging a memory track in all of them.

The interaction between the child and its mother as well as with its father, becomes a prototype for close relations, teaching the child how to attract and give attention. The child learns how to make attachments in close relations, with all that entails for better or worse.

The problems caused by projective identification can stem from the lack of developed personal boundaries. The resultant ambiguity regarding the involved people's feelings and intentions, sooner or later, gives rise to unintentional or unforeseen consequences.

My own interaction with my mother was one of insecurity and avoidance and when that finally dawned on me, I could clearly understand my own behavior in close relationships.

It was an epiphany for me, when I finally understood the answer to the mystery that I had posed myself.

It's impossible to specify objective FRAMES-reality because we can't measure dynamic experiences objectively. However, subjective experiences we have of ourselves can be analyzed using the FRAMES model.

Both you and I can ask ourselves the existential question of how objective our subjective experiences are.

The comprehensive answer to that question is that, we are all unique and that our subjective realities cannot be measured or compared, objectively.

I am the eighth-born of eleven siblings. When I looked back on the interaction I had with my mother, I wondered what self-perceptions my mother had and how that affected her interaction with me.

I know that the circumstances in my family changed radically a few years before I was born.

After realizing this I soon had a dream that formed my reflections.

In the dream, having had prepared the "funeral" of my childhood perspective of my parents as inner objects, I could re-establish them as heroes, seen in the light of reflections, later in life.

I felt liberated and relaxed with my parents as inner objects.

If an individual has experienced attachment issues early in life, it may hinder the recognition and establishment of healthy attachments later on in life.

An early distortion in the child's subject relations, can have consequences for who it subsequently chooses as a partner in early adulthood.

Mutual feelings of attachment in a close relationship require that both partners are capable of receiving love while at the same time being able to give love.

When we wish to understand how our psyche works or when a therapist wants to build a comprehensive appraisal of a patient, thinking in a cyclical fashion is important because psyche and relationships function cyclically (reciprocally).

However, if we wish to achieve change, we may need to think lineally, with a step-by-step vision for change.

What is the necessary first step to achieve the change we desire?

What is essential to stay on the path to change?

What is imperative in order to break free from re-occurring behavioral patterns that we want to extricate ourselves from?

How should we behave in a close relationship if we strive for genuine contact/interaction?

Is it characterized by an open and honest, mutual interaction?

To some extent it depends on the experiences both had of the forging of attachments in childhood.

The (subconscious) recognition of traits or events experienced in relationships earlier in life can make it easy for us to fall for someone who reminds us of influential people from the past.

Not finding this sense of recognition can lead to a feeling of being lost in the relationship.

The following matrix is a compilation of how attachment between young adults can be formed in different ways depending on whether the partners behave immaturely and egocentrically or they take equal responsibility for an open communication.

Personal behavior leads to consequences in how the subject is treated by the object. If A expects reciprocity but B behaves egocentrically, then A risks becoming disappointed.

	Individual A	
	Egocentric attachment-behavior in A	Mutual attachment action in A
Egocentric attachment-behavior in B	Mutual ego-centricity	Risk of disappointment with A
Mutual attachment action in B	Risk of disappointment with B	Probable success in the interaction

Individual B

If only one of the partners makes the effort to adapt, there's a risk that the Perls´ ideal of maintaining self-respect will not be realized and ultimately that personal boundaries in the relationship cannot be kept.

Poor psychological health can be related to all of the five FRAME parameters: perception, stress, behavior, reflection and expression of our feelings.

The majority of youths seeking psychological support at the health center were mostly affected by stress related psychological ill-health.

The development of personal boundaries and independence occurs predominantly during the teenage years.

Parents and children can each have mixed feelings about the child's independence.

The opportunity of achieving freedom can be alluring while the risk of feeling alone can be construed as threatening.

Our strongest emotions are associated with relationships and attachment: Reunions, goodbyes, sorrow and yearning, intimacy, jealousy and shared joy.

We experience a multiplicity of emotions. They are derived from different situations, associated with different perceptions and diverse thoughts.

The two juxtaposed effects that the amygdala centra in the cerebrum (where emotional responses are processed) have on the psyche can elicit the whole gamut of emotions from hate to love.

When we act and think during our interaction with someone, we feel differently depending on the situation and the relationship we have with the person we are interacting with.

Benevolence and malevolence in our emotional lives are connected to the amygdala's activity.

Our feelings on a scale between benevolence and malevolence are conditioned by our externally tuned senses (sight, hearing, smell, taste and touch) and our intrinsic sensory perceptions (interoception).

This combination of extrinsic and intrinsic sensory perceptions is related to selectively directed attention and confirmation bias.

Seeing or hearing something that evokes inner stress or reluctance leads us to resist comprehending it.

Freud, logically coined the term defense mechanism to describe this problem. It's as if we are fitted with an auditory filter and tunnel vision that protects us from experiences that we can't reconcile with how we think or feel.

When the information we gather, while communicating with a relation object, is deficient, we are inclined to fill in the missing information with our own thinking and misconstrue the spirit and vibe of what is being said.

This mechanism is heightened in groups with a strong bond, whose members cut themselves off from the outside world.

In this book, it is my wish to describe a new biologically, socially and psychologically based system theory of attachment between people, not only with an acting subject but also with an object of attachment.

Material objects in our midst can "inspire" and evoke strong emotions within us.

I have had strong feelings for the guitar I had in my youth that I carried with me wherever I went. It was an emotionally charged object of transition during my teenage years.

I have an affinity for and understanding of indigenous peoples wish to give spirit to and be inspired by natural phenomena. They regard some places as sacred.

The Pharoah and his subservient elites of Egyptian culture, worshipped the Sun god, thus giving the sun a spirit and animating it.

Even some of our contemporary gatherings are regarded as sacred for some people. The moose hunt, religious ceremonies, market and musical festivals and so on, are all examples of this.

Actors who have portrayed characters in tv-series and become objects of projection, can be assigned personal traits that might not necessarily correspond with how they are in real life.

When you project feelings onto something, whether they are living or inanimate objects, you experience a feeling via your inner senses (interoception), at the same time as you are aware of phenomena around you via your external senses (perception).

In the beginning of life when the small child experiences its mother, it experiences both its own body and its mother´s. In other words, it experiences a dichotomy of intrinsic and extrinsic sensory perceptions.

As time goes by, there is an accumulation of experiences of independence and experiences of parents as permanent inner objects, i.e. experiences of the boundaries between oneself and one´s parents as relation object.

This eventually leads us to perceive ourselves as individuals in our own right, with our own identity and integrity.

Young people gradually become more proficient at managing their opposing feelings towards mam and dad. The degree of success they have in this regard, depends on the situation and how their emotional status is at the time.

In an adult relationship, experiences of object permanence can develop due to a growing sense of security in the relationship. This is made possible through effective, genuine and honest communication between both partners.

Communicating emotions is best done "in real life", when both partners are present in the same situation and are experiencing how the other acts, their body-language and tone of voice, given the particular set of circumstances they find themselves in, at that specific point in time.

Epilogue

On a British talk-show, Rowan Atkinson talked about when he failed to convince a guard at a parking house that he was the "real" Mr. Bean.

The host and audience were left, bent over laughing. Rowan Atkinson needs only to show his countenance to amuse most of us.

The parking guard: "You´re the image of Mr. Bean!"

Rowan Atkinson: "I am Mr. Bean!"

The parking guard: "You could make a fortune as his double"

We never really got to find out if the parking guard was persuaded that Atkinson wasn't really only a double.

Rowan Atkinson was ascribed a confusing projection of his external, physical identity as Mr. Bean.

It's even more troublesome having the projection of an inner identity thrust upon you, which presumably is all about other´s conceptions, as subjects.

Most people who have an official role in society, communicating with people, such as politicians, teachers, priests etc. can be assigned the projections of other people's inner spirituality.

This is even more confusing because inner identities are not apparent externally, in the same way.

In a loyal, well-knit group, people can convince each other that they are exactly the same by using some exterior symbol or uniform.

Human communication can be hindered or even totally blocked due to the influence of the mechanisms of projection, identification and defence.

An example of this is in political debates, when a politician focusses on the intentions of the adversary instead of using debate time to present his/her own opinions and wishes in different political issues.

This can easily lead to projective identification and a distorted view of the adversary and subsequent systemic consequences as a result.

It also increases the risk of focusing on something to substantiate one's own prejudices.

A good example of projecting onto your antagonist instead of owning your own negative feelings is when upset school-mates defend themselves by saying: "It was his fault, he was the one who started it!".

Mutual projective identification stems from fragile subject relations, where people are likely to regard each other with the perception of their own prejudicially, colored eye-glasses.

Idols can be viewed as perfect even though those who don't idolize them can see that they have normal human reactions and behavior.

This illustrates the importance of increasing our awareness of how selectively directed attention and projective identification occurs within us, i.e., how confirmation bias and labelling of others functions.

My musical colleague, Sverker Belin, who wrote "Relation före Metod", confirmed my observation that object relation theorists highlight the reciprocal effect between an acting individual's perspective and the perspective of a person who is the object of strong positive or negative feelings.

Freud's interest in the specific case of triangulation that he named the Oedipus complex, shows us the complex nature of triangulation brought on by an ambiguity about who wants to do what with whom, especially in the case of triangulation between mother, father and child.

On the occasions that I had warped negative projections assigned to me, I have felt despondent. I've felt as though I've been snared in a drama triangle between myself, the other person and that persons' inner notion of who I am.

Sometimes it feels like it doesn't make a difference what I say. In desperation, I sometimes say that "I think I know what you mean and I think you don't understand what I mean".

When a person tries to make himself understood we might not understand the words that are actually used or the spirit in which they are being said.

Human communication is all about the exchange of opinions on what we perceive, how we react to its content, what we want to do with the knowledge it brings and finally, how we think and feel about it all.

Obviously, there can be problems with transference and counter-transference of feelings towards someone else, not only in therapeutical relations but also in everyday social situations.

To those who have problems with an angry neighbor, think of it this way; you have to be able to control your counter-projection on your neighbor, as well as his probable aggravation with you.

My clinical experience in the field of pure family therapy is pretty limited compared to all the years I spent working on investigations and therapy sessions.

However, the family background of my clients has always been a central part in my thinking in the therapy sessions I've had about relationships.

I have concluded that information about the psychophysiology of anxiety as well as analysis of relational and existential questions are central in the therapy process.

Sometimes, I wonder why certain experiences we have about ourselves can be so hard to push away. When this happens, I construct a FRAMES-trap, imagined symbolically as the weave in a willow basket. The young flexible twigs can symbolize growth in the five psychophysiological lines of development; selectively directed attention, physiological reactions, social action, reflections and emotions.

I also imagine that the trap causes a mental block and is perpetuated in certain social contexts.

Some FRAMES-traps are more difficult to unlock than others.

As life goes on and we gain better insight, experience and maturity, we tend to get better at emancipating ourselves from the mental blocks that we had in the past.

The young are only beginning their journey into life and it is my wish that by helping them improve their knowledge about themselves, they will find a steady base to stand on and an appreciation of life.

I feel privileged to have been able to work with young people and can certainly agree with an expression I've heard used by teachers in primary school: "You learn as long as you have students".

References

Baldwin, A.L. (1967) Theories of Child Development. A Wiley International Edition.

Belin, S. (2020) Relation före Metod. Dualis.

Brehmer, B. & Garpebring, S. Social pressure and policy change in the "lens model", interpesonal conflict paradigm. Scand. J. Psychology., 1974, 15, 191-196.

Cullberg Weston, M. (2008) Från skam till självrespekt. Natur & Kultur.

Garpebring, S. (2014) Stressreflexer och tankefällor. Nomen Förlag.

Garpebring, S. (2016) Fokus och Bakgrund. Books on Demand.

Garpebring, S. (2018) En psykologisk Rammodell. Books on Demand – En reviderad version av FRAME: S en psykologisk rammodell (2004).

Garpebring, S. (2020) Identitet inifrån – Upplevelser av sig själv. Books on Demand.

Garpebring, S. (2020) Var sin psykologi – Om individualitet i relationer. Books on Demand.

Garpebring, S. (2021) Vetande om sig själv. Books on Demand.

Hansen, A. (2016) Hjärnstark. Fitnessförlaget.

Harari, Y. N. (2017) Homo Deus. Natur & Kultur. Swedish Audio Book.

Hendricks, G. & K. (1995) Kroppens egen intelligens. Svenska Dagbladets Förlags AB.

Lejonöga, C. & Lilja Ljung, A. (2018) Leva nu: om trauma & dissociation. Recito Förlag.

Li, W. (2019) Eat to beat disease. Grand Central Publishing.

Malmström, C. (2003) Stress i Psykosomatik. www.medicallink.se

Solms, M. (2021) The Source of Consciousness. YouTube – The Royal Institution.

Seth, A. (2017) The Neuroscience of Consciousness. Level/ Content/ Self. YouTube – The Royal Institution.

Tomm, K. (2000) Systemisk intervjumetodik. Bokförlaget Mareld.